Homework
Sucks

www.transworldbooks.co.uk

Also by Simon Mayo

Confessions

Itch

HOMEWORK SUCKS!

A *Drivetime* Book of Really
Useful Information

SIMON MAYO

BANTAM PRESS

LONDON · TORONTO · SYDNEY · AUCKLAND · JOHANNESBURG

TRANSWORLD PUBLISHERS
61–63 Uxbridge Road, London W5 5SA
A Random House Group Company
www.transworldbooks.co.uk

First published in Great Britain
in 2012 by Bantam Press
an imprint of Transworld Publishers

A CIP catalogue record for this book
is available from the British Library.

ISBN 9780593069479

For my daughter Natasha, who loves homework so much

Contents

Introduction

There comes a moment in most parents' lives when you suddenly realize how little you remember about your schooling. The friends, foes and teachers you recall with no trouble at all. The buildings, the smells and the food can fill your senses still and you can be back in assembly or the dining room in an instant. It's the education bit that's fraying at the edges. You find yourself trying to come up with an answer for Junior without resorting to Prof. Google or Dr Wikipedia, and failing.

There is pride at stake, of course. All your child's life you have been asked questions like, 'Why is the sky blue?', 'Where do dreams come from?', 'Why do men have nipples?' Each time you have answered to the best of your ability, but as your child gets older, it is with less confidence than before. You detect the flicker of doubt in your offspring. Maybe it's their stance – arms folded, head on one side. Maybe it's the narrowing of their eyes, the time-honoured reflex of the doubtful. Or maybe it's hearing, 'You're talking rubbish, Dad. That's not what Miss Johnson says at all.' This is usually accompanied with a world-weary shrug (where *did* they learn that?) and a slow walk away, the trudge of disappointment. If you also get the reproachful glance over the shoulder, you've had the complete works. The full monty. Welcome to the club.

You might have imagined that if your kids got to university,

that would be the time when you'd be no use to them (academically
– not financially, clearly). Or maybe the upper reaches of the
secondary school would be when you had to bail out. What you
never, ever realized was that you would run out of answers *while
they were still at primary school.*

So you have this book just in time.

You might not hold on to the crown of 'all-knowing-parent'
for very much longer, but you could keep it in your anxious hands
for a little while yet. All you need to do is learn the contents
of this book by heart and personalize each answer. This way
it sounds as though you really do know what you are talking
about.

Of course we – and by this I am making the huge assumption
that you are one of the great tribe of the middle-aged – are
at a great disadvantage here, one not really understood by the
younger generation. It is that we never really had homework,
not like they do now. Most of us never got any homework
till secondary school. Now you have parents fighting to find
the nursery most likely to give their delightful toddler compul-
sory computing and Mandarin twice a day. If they're not
reading Proust for fun (and in the original French, obviously)
by year one primary, someone will need to be sacked. 'One hour
of algebra, is that all?' seems to be the mood, so extra tutors
have to be found to fill the gap left so neglectfully by the school
system.

Your alternative is to wield this book with wisdom and
judgement.

The internet has, of course, transformed the homework
experience. This can be a godsend, for them and for us. You
can instantly have the knowledge of the ages appear on your
screen, and in no time you know the capital of Uzbekistan,

the longest novel in the world and the Latin for 'Beware of the dog'. (Tashkent, *In Search of Lost Time* by Proust – yes, him again – and '*Cave canem*'.) Equally, your screen can fill up with preposterous nonsense and mindless distractions. And so can theirs. And the chances are their distractions are more mindless than yours. Ridiculous as it might sound, there are some things you can't really Google. There are some occasions when you have to ask someone who might actually Have Gone Out And Done Something. Once upon a time you could ask the elders of the village; now you can ask the Radio 2 *Drivetime* audience. They manage to balance wisdom and cool, wit and erudition and Simon & Garfunkel. That's my kind of town.

What sparked this radio feature was a walk on the beach with Child 2, who was complaining about the amount of school work she had to do that week. 'Homework sucks!' was her cry, and I thought that sounded a great title. (I was concerned for her workload, too, but when an idea takes you . . .) Originally I had thought of TV but when the Radio 2 call came it seemed a perfect fit. Previous *Drivetime* host John Dunn had a feature called 'Answers Please' and Chris Evans had 'Fox the Fox', so this was another tradition I thought was worth upholding. The definition of what homework is has broadened considerably and now takes in anything you can't work out on your own. Life in general, basically. Many of my favourite queries are here: 'chunking' in maths, why races go anti-clockwise and how different would the world be if it spun in the opposite direction? These are brilliant questions and I hope you enjoy reading the answers (and then learning them. See above). There will be a test after lunch.

There is a clever chapter at the end with no answers. We thought you might like to join in with that one, and it saves us some time. Tweet us your best ideas using the hashtag #homeworksucks!

Thanks to the whole *Drivetime* crew who assemble the show lovingly each day. Gary Bones, Fiona Day, Mark Plant, Joe Haddon and Ben Backhouse – take a bow. Curtsey. Shuffle a bit, look embarrassed and leave.

And thanks for listening, buying and reading. Here's to knowing stuff!

'WHO DECIDED THAT AN HOUR IS AN HOUR?'

Mind-Boggling Maths

Simon,

I share my birthday with my handsome husband and his brother – we were born in different years, but all on the same day.

What's the likelihood of three closely linked people sharing the same birthday? And how many people would you need to encounter to make a mutual birthday a probability?

CLARICE in Leeds

JONATHAN from Ludlow
Maths tutor

If you take three people at random, there's only a 0.00075 per cent chance that they will share the same birthday. But it would take just 23 people in a room to make it more likely than not that two of them would have a mutual birthday.

With 41 people, the probability increases to over 90 per cent, and with 57 people it's 99 per cent.

Simon,

I made a cake with two friends. I cut it into three equal pieces, a third for each of us.

My question is, why can't I represent any one of these pieces as a whole number in mathematics? If the whole of the cake is 100 per cent, then why is the sum of the 3 slices 99.999 per cent recurring?

Where has that other bit of cake gone?!

FRANK in Whitstable

CARRIE from Reading
Engineer

We use decimals, which is a nominal way of measuring. The recurring symbol is an illustration of the perfect fraction; 0.9 recurring equals 1.0, so there's no cake missing!

> Simon,
>
> *With the commodity markets showing an increase in the value of scrap metal, and assuming current interest and inflation rates, how soon will a two-pence piece actually be worth more as scrap metal than as a coin of the realm?*
>
> **STEVE** in High Wycombe

PHIL
From Coin News *magazine*

Pre-1992, when 2ps were 97 per cent copper, it would have been worthwhile. Now, it's a copper-steel alloy. A two-pence piece weighs 7.1 grams, so you would need 140,449 coins – or £2,808.98 – to get a tonne. With a tonne currently worth $435, that would not be a good pay-off. I should stress it is illegal to melt money!

Simon,

Why is the '4' on a clock face with Roman numerals shown as four 'I's when it should be 'IV'? After all, number 6 is shown as 'VI'. No one I've asked seems to know – perhaps you can help.

DAVID in Leigh

RICHARD from Bridport
Antique-clock restorer

Possibly for aesthetic reasons: 'IIII' is used instead of 'IV' to balance the clock face, as in the same position on the opposite side is 8, or 'VIII'. It's also possible that the 'IIII' was used by chance in the old days, and people were so poorly educated at the time that no one raised an objection, and thus the 'IIII' became standard. Interestingly, I know of two – only two – clock faces that use the 'IV', one of which is the Tower Clock, in other words, the Big Ben clock.

> Simon,
>
> My partner Liam has an MP3 player, which he loves. He has about 4,000 tracks on it, and plays it for around 40 minutes per day on shuffle – so, about 12 tracks a day. So how is it that he repeatedly hears either the same tracks or the same artist within days?
>
> **SARAH** in Nottingham

SPENCER from London
Presents 'Click' on BBC World News

First of all, there's no such thing as 'random' for computers. Also, if you're syncing every evening, your shuffle resets, so it's not unlikely that the same songs will come around. Or it might be that the MP3 player is choosing songs or artists that you favour, either through previous plays or ratings.

> *Simon,*
>
> *We all know the speed of sound and light . . .
> but what is the speed of this text or email?*
>
> **STUART** *in Hatfield*

MITTAL from Elstree
*Engineer at a secure systems company, with a background
in avionics engineering and transmissions analysis*

Texts and emails travel at the speed of light (3×10^8
m/second), but will be slowed down by a number of
variables:

- the number of relays (supervised and
  unsupervised – add 1 or 2 seconds for each);
- the transmission speed of the handset
  (if a text);
- the network being used (for both emails and
  texts);
- electromagnetic interference in the
  atmosphere.

International texts and emails do take longer, because
they have more and higher security relays to get
through.

> Simon,
>
> *I'm always amazed at songwriters' ability to come up with totally new melodies. Given that there are a finite number of notes, is there a limit to the number of totally new melodies that can be written?*
>
> *Many thanks!*
>
> ### RICHARD in Norwich

GAVIN from Cambridge
Director of music at a secondary school

For just a five-note melody you'd have 64 x 64 x 64 x 64 x 64 permutations, which equals just over 1 billion. Create a whole tune and the number of permutations is indeed both frightening and overwhelming, which perhaps explains why it is hard for a composer to write a new tune that is both appealing and memorable. It's not something that 'anyone can do'!

Simon,

Why do runners competing in races such as the 100 metres, 200 metres, etc., run anti-clockwise around a running track, whereas with horse-racing or motor-racing the race can be run either way?

FERGAL in Burnley

MIKE from London
BBC Radio 5 Live's athletics correspondent

Apparently, it all dates back to the 1908 Olympic Games. Running tracks have been standardized since the revival of the Olympics, in order to create a system where world records can be achieved. The shape and size of the track, as well as the direction the runners race in, are also standardized.

Hello Simon – just wondering . . .

Given that there is a direct relationship between engine revolutions and the rotation of the driven wheels on a car, if I were to attach four-times bigger wheels to my car, would fuel consumption drop by a quarter?

CHARLIE in Gourock

DONALD from Newcastle
Mechanic

If anything, having bigger wheels will increase fuel consumption, because the engine will have to work harder to get through the gears. Think of it like a bike – the smaller the cog at the back in relation to the wheel, the harder you have to pedal.

Simon,

My 8-year-old son had some long division this weekend for homework. However, they are now taught a method called 'chunking'. Can you please explain how to long-divide using chunking?

I wish someone could also explain why it is that methods for learning basic maths keep changing every generation, making it such a challenge for parents to help their children!

PHILIPPA in Hook

CRAIG from Bath
Head of maths

Chunking is division as repeated subtraction. It came in with the national numeracy strategy a few years ago, which introduced techniques to build on what the kids already knew. Example: 567 divided by 7. Multiply 7 by 10 then subtract from 567. Repeat until you can't do it any more! It goes like this:

567 minus 70 = 497 (so that's 10 sevens you've taken away)
497 minus 70 = 427 (that's 20 sevens you've taken away)
427 minus 70 = 357 (that's 30 sevens . . .)
357 minus 70 = 287 (40 sevens . . .)
287 minus 70 = 217 (50 sevens . . .)
217 minus 70 = 147 (60 sevens . . .)
147 minus 70 = 77 (70 sevens . . .)

77 minus 70 = 7, so that's 80 sevens you've taken away, and you've got 1 seven left, and 80 + 1 = 81, which means there are 81 sevens in 567. In other words: 567 divided by 7 equals 81.

> Simon,
>
> *Why on earth are the numbers on a computer keyboard the other way up to those on a telephone keypad? Why is the keyboard top to bottom – 789, 456, 123 – rather than 123, 456, 789?*
>
> *Thanks!*
>
> **PETER** *from Welford*

NICK from Verwood

Electronics engineer who spent many years specializing in the repair of office telephones

When telephone keypads were being developed in the late 1950s, pulses were still used to connect to lines at the telephone exchange, with '0' requiring ten pulses and the '1' requiring one pulse. Office personnel were used to the layout of adding machines and calculators, whose top row was 789 – a layout that computer keyboards were to follow – and regular users were extremely fast at data entry. Therefore, the order on the new telephone keypad was inverted, with 123 along the top, to slow down the dialling process among practised users and allow the pulses to catch up.

That's one theory. Another is that the telephone keypad was designed to be familiar to people who were used to entering the number on a rotary dial. (Interesting that we still talk about 'dialling' a phone number, long since we ceased to use dials!) On a rotary dial, the number 1 was at the top, so it made sense for the new touch pad to start with 1 at the top too.

Simon,

Can you please explain 'surds' to me? It's my daughter's year-10 maths homework. Apparently, they're based around square roots, supposedly a way of expressing irrational numbers that can't be broken down to simple decimals or fractions. What possible use would they be in real life?

Thanking you!

ANN *from* Poole

JAMES from Nottingham
Maths teacher

A surd is an irrational number (i.e. a number with no square root) presented in a more manageable form. So, for instance, the surd of the square root of twenty is four lots of the square root of five. They are very useful in lots of areas, including measurements. Basically, if you can't simplify a number to remove a square root, it's a surd. And their decimals go on for ever!

> Simon,
>
> *Driving on the M25 the other day, I wondered how much further I would travel if I did a complete circuit in the slow lane clockwise (i.e. the outermost lane) than if I did a complete circuit in the slow lane anti-clockwise (i.e. the innermost lane)?*
>
> *Many thanks!*
>
> **GRAHAM** in West Sussex

ROBERT

HGV driver who has driven both ways round for charity

It's very hard to calculate the exact distance saved mathematically, as the M25 is not a perfect circle. However, driving both ways round – once in the outermost lane, and once in the innermost lane – shows that you save about a tenth of a mile in the innermost lane.

> Simon,
>
> How many normal party-sized balloons filled with helium would it take to lift a man of average build (say 5 foot 11 and 12 stone – or 1.8 metres and 75 kilograms) in the style of the film Up?
>
> Thanks!
>
> **PETER** in Spain

KYLA from Malmesbury
Helium balloon decorator

A standard balloon will lift around 9 grams of weight. This means that it would take 7,055 balloons to lift me, and 8,333 balloons to raise the average 75kg man into the skies.

> Simon,
>
> *I've been puzzling over this one for a while now. There are 24 hours in a day, 7 days in a week, 52 weeks in a year and 365 days in a regular year (not a leap year).*
>
> *So how come if you multiply 7 days in a week by 52 weeks in a year the total is 364, not 365? Where does the extra day come from?*
>
> **MICK** in West Sussex

LIZZY
Science teacher in Godalming

The day has not 'come' from anywhere. It exists since it takes 365 days and 6 hours for the earth to make a complete orbit of the sun. A day is defined as 24 hours since that is how long it takes the earth to turn once on its axis. So the answer to the question, Mick, is that you are right – there aren't exactly 52 weeks in a year from 1 January to 31 December: there are 52 weeks and a day, except in a leap year, when there are 52 weeks and 2 days.

> *Simon,*
>
> *The Olympic running events go from 100 metres to 200 metres, 400 metres to 800 metres. A nice straightforward progression and each distance fits nicely around a 400-metre running track. There is then a leap to 1500 metres (3¾ laps) – why?*
>
> *It may be to avoid the imperial mile, but four laps of a metric track would still be 1600 metres and would be more logical. Or is it that 1600 metres converts to about 1750 yards, which was too close to a mile for Baron Coubertin's French sensibilities?*
>
> *Does anyone have the explanation, please?*
>
> **IAN** in Dunfermline

PHILIP
Olympics historian

It's not entirely clear, but it seems the most likely explanation is compromise. In Europe they had 500-metre tracks, whereas here and in the US they stuck to the imperial mile with 440-yard tracks. When they needed to standardize, 1,500 – or three laps of a 500-metre track – was closest to the imperial mile in the metric system.

> Hi Simon,
>
> My son Marcus, aged 10, is very good at maths, but a question that's stumping him at the moment is what's zero divided by zero? Is it 1, O or infinity?
>
>   It seems an easy question on the surface – anything divided by itself is surely 1. But then anything divided by O is usually O.
>
>   So what's the right answer?
>
> **JAN** in Hereford

JULIE from Oxford
Cambridge maths graduate

 It's often described as 'undefined', but it's infinity because of the way fractions work. Divide 2 by $\frac{1}{2}$ and it becomes 4. Divide 2 by $\frac{1}{10}$ and it becomes 20 – and so on, ever closer to infinity. The same works in reverse when you divide fractions by fractions!

> Simon,
>
> *My daughter Katherine was home poorly recently, and spent the day quizzing me on a myriad of subjects, one of which was quite interesting. Who decided that an hour is an hour, and how did they decide?*
>
> **RACHEL** in West Cornwall

CHARLES
Horologist

The Mesopotamians came up with it. They had a counting system based on 12 and 60, and they used the same system to work out the divisions by which to measure time.

> *Dear Simon,*
>
> *When wrapping presents, is there a mathematical/ scientific approach that optimizes the use of wrapping paper? i.e., square on, at an angle, and so on?*
>
> **WILLIAM** in Wishaw

JANE
Gift-wrapping expert

Here are four ways to get the most coverage out of your wrapping paper.

1. Have as little overlap as possible.
2. If you have two odd bits of leftover paper, combine them to wrap a larger present, and make it look 'arty'.
3. Choose non-Christmas specific paper so that the leftover paper can be used throughout the year.
4. Use tissue paper, cellophane or flexible wrapping for unusually shaped presents.

Simon,

I was recently reading about Alexander the Great, and that he was born in 356 BC, which made me wonder what year it would have been to the people who lived at the time, as they obviously couldn't have called it 356 BC . . .

What calendar system was in place back then?

Thank you!

NIGEL in Consett

KARINA, aged 13, from Teesside
A student who loves history

According to a book by Mitchell Symons I've read, the answer is:

Using the Roman calendar:	397
Using the Old Testament calendar:	3648

Simon,

Who decided the sequence of the numbers on a dartboard? Is there any logic to it?

Thanks!

STEVE in **Ripley**

BARRY from Birmingham
Who runs an oche-supply company

The game of darts is thought to date back to medieval times and the sport of archery, but the board as we know it is credited to Lancashire carpenter Brian Gamlin, who positioned the numbers so as to penalize inaccuracy.

> Simon,
>
> When can you reuse a calendar and get the right days/dates? With leap years and the like it is difficult to work out when a 'repeat' year happens. I always save my picture calendars, and I'd like to be able to use them again when accurate.
>
> Thanks!
>
> ### *JANE* in Cranleigh

JANET from Horsham
Who ran a '2000 project' dealing with the computer changeover at the new millennium

You can reuse the calendar of any year that has the same number of days and the same starting weekday. Leap-year calendars are reusable every 28 years; non-leap-year calendars are reusable every six or eleven years. Holidays – such as Easter – won't match exactly, however. The newest calendar you could have reused for 2012 (a leap year) was 1984, and the next time you could reuse it would be 2040. For 2013 you could reuse a calendar from 2002, 1991, 1985 or 1974 (to give the four most recent), and you can use the same one in 2019. In 2014 you can get out your old 2003, 1997, 1986 or 1975 calendars, and you can keep it for use again in 2025.

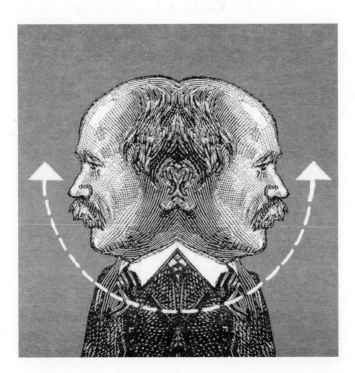

'WHY DO WE NOD AND SHAKE OUR HEADS?'

Cultural Conundrums

> *Dear Simon,*
>
> *My daughter has come up with what I hope you and the team consider an interesting question. What would happen if William and Kate have twins? Who would be first in line for succession to the throne? Would it be the midwife's decision as to who is delivered first?*
>
> *Perhaps one of your listeners can help.*
>
> **ANNE** in Olney

LUCINDA from Sandwich
Midwife

Twins are called 'twin one' and 'twin two' in utero, depending on their position in the womb. Twin one will come out first during natural birth, as it is lower. When it comes to C-section, it's whichever one the surgeon can get to most easily – so it's not a matter of choice.

Simon,

Where do wedding anniversary meanings come from? For example, paper, wood, silver, ruby, gold . . .

Are they throwbacks to ancient rituals, or were they invented by card manufacturers?

Thank you!

JULIA

SARAH
Wedding planner

The tradition is thought to have originated in medieval Germany where, if a married couple lived to celebrate the twenty-fifth anniversary of their wedding, the wife was presented by friends with a silver wreath. On celebration of the fiftieth – properly extraordinary in those days! – the wife received a wreath of gold. Over time the number of symbols expanded in different cultures. Retail has had something to do with it too.

Simon,

Why are badge logos and pockets always on the left side of shirts?

DAVE in Carlisle

LISA from Abergavenny
Tailoress

Logos and badges are on the left so they are near to your heart, pledging allegiance to your team/club/company! You could trace it back to medieval times, when knights held their shields on the left to protect their heart.

> *Simon,*
>
> *When you buy a house, you own the house and any gardens associated with it – but how much of the land below the house do you own?*
>
> **LEE** in Pocklington

DAVID from Whitby
Chartered surveyor

 You own right down to the middle of the earth and all the sky above it. The slight problem is that you don't have mineral rights to anything beneath you, and you'd need planning permission to build down, which you probably wouldn't get.

Dear Simon,

*I have 27 first cousins – children of my parents'
brothers and sisters, and my husband has two
cousins, from his father's half brother and sister.*

*I was wondering if there was such a thing as
a 'step cousin?' And that got me thinking about
'second cousins' and who they are exactly, which
then got me started on 'second cousins once
removed'!*

*I'm in a bit of a muddle and thought one
of your highly intelligent listeners may be
able to help.*

JUDITH in Reading

PAUL from Dulwich
Genealogist

It's really quite simple. First cousins have the same
grandparents. Second cousins have the same great-
grandparents. Third cousins have the same great-
great-grandparents. 'Once removed' are their offspring
or parents – in other words, they are one generation
above or below.

Simon and team,

I have a question about Jimmy Buffett's classic song, 'It's Five O'Clock Somewhere'. In the chorus, Buffett sings that it might be only half past twelve where he is, but it's five o'clock somewhere in the world, and he wants a drink! Assuming I am in Nashville and it is in fact 12.30, is it actually five o'clock somewhere, and could you legally be served a drink there?

MIKE from West Yorkshire

GRANT from Worthing
BA cabin crew member

For it to be exactly five o'clock somewhere, you'd need to be in a country that has half-hour time zones. In my job I go to many different time zones, and I can tell you there are very few half-hour ones. Adelaide in Australia is one, but 12.30 p.m. in Nashville (summer time) would be 3 a.m. in Adelaide, so that's no good. India is another country with half-hour zones, but it would be 11 p.m. there. Close to hitting the right time spot, with the additional benefit of generous licensing laws – is us! So never mind Nashville, try Nottingham instead.

Simon,

My niece Hallie asked me this at the weekend:
if an 18-year-old got on a flight to the USA, at
which point during the flight would they not get
served alcohol under American law? When does
UK law stop and US law begin? Mid-flight? When
it touches down? As soon as the doors close?

Please tell us!!

STEVE in Southend-on-Sea

MATTHEW from Reigate
Lawyer

The law that applies is that of the flag of the vessel.
That is, if the aircraft is registered in the UK, then
UK laws apply. If registered in the USA, US laws
apply. It's not about the airline, and it's certainly not
a matter of where the aeroplane is flying over at the
time!

Simon,

I have been wondering for a while now: when did people start putting an 'upstairs' in houses? Years and years ago people lived in caves and mud huts, which were only one level. I'm not sure why, but at some point someone must have thought to put a second level in their house – and it was obviously a popular idea.

I hope you can help . . .

EMMA

CHRIS from Glasgow
Been on a dig on Santorini

The Minoans on Santorini had two-storey houses, and they were around in 4,000 BC! It is also thought that the Sumer civilization (in what is now Iraq) also built two-storey houses. It is likely that in both cases only the very rich made use of two-storey houses – the poor would probably have lived in simple huts.

Dear Simon,

We recently purchased some new Christmas decorations for the office, blowing most of the budget on a set of electric blue lights.

After turning the lights on, we noticed one of the lights was white. This prompted much discussion among my colleagues. Thinking back, it occurred to me that all the lights I've ever owned have included a single white light – usually at the start of the set. I've never known why – can someone shed some 'light' on this, please?

JOHN in Cardiff

TERRY from Hilburton
Former refrigerator engineer

The first bulb in the string is a fuse bulb. It has a slightly thinner filament which blows in a surge – to protect the rest of the bulbs.

Dear Simon,

I work as a vicar in Moston, Manchester. I am preaching this Christmas and I need a new angle. I have stood there with a tea towel on my head, holding a doll and pretending to be Joseph. I have rollerbladed around the church showing that God stepped into our shoes to show us how to be more fully human. I have talked about Jesus as the Light of the World, and how, being born in a stable and not a palace, he made himself accessible to rich and poor, wise men and shepherds alike.

This is my eleventh Christmas in this post, and although there is a temptation to recycle, I would much rather offer something fresh.

Can you and your listeners help?

REV. MATT in Manchester

ANDY in Stanmore
Pastor

We have a tree in the church upon which people have been putting their prayers in little envelopes. On Christmas day, with everyone's permission, we're taking the envelopes down and reading all the prayers out.

Dear Simon,

*My twin boys will be 21 in March, and I'm
trying to think of a suitably auspicious twenty-first
birthday present for the twenty-first century. A
watch or something similar doesn't quite seem to
cut it – plus I don't want to spend a fortune, as
money is tight!*

Thanks for your help.

JANE

KATE from Coulsdon
Whose son Jake was 21 last March

My husband and I paid for my son Jake and his
friends to see Crystal Palace at Selhurst Park. We also
gave the club a donation to allow Jake to be Crystal
Palace's mascot, Pete the Eagle, during half-time.
And Jake's sister Sarah put together a Life Book of
photographs, stories, memories and anecdotes from
friends, teachers and relatives.

> Simon,
>
> *What are the origins of nodding and shaking your head as alternatives to saying yes and no?*
>
> **PAUL** in Bristol

JULES from Colchester
Married to a man who reads Desmond Morris

I was discussing it with my husband at the weekend, who had just read about this very question in a Desmond Morris book. It's all to do with how babies suckle. When babies have finished, they turn their head to the side – meaning no! When they want more they lean forward – effectively nodding. That's one theory anyway!

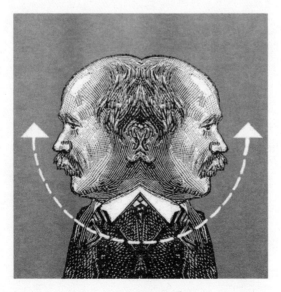

Hi Simon,

My daughter Lara is getting married in the summer, and the whole mother-of-the-bride outfit-thing is beginning to worry me. I am in my forties, and I don't want to look a) like something out of Footballers' Wives, or b) like a dowager duchess.

I've already trawled shops, magazines and the web for inspiration, but to no avail. I'm now looking to you for inspiration – help!

Many thanks!

JACKI in Lincolnshire

CLARE, near Lavenham

Designer and couture dressmaker, specializing in bridal wear

These are the things to remember:

- The mother of the bride is just as important as the bride herself – but it's very important for her not to outdo the bride!
- Pay a visit to a reputable dressmaker who will be able to advise, taking into account your shape, colouring and, most importantly, budget.
- Take your best friend and/or daughter with you – somebody you trust to give an honest opinion and to help with any suggestions made by the dressmaker.
- Be true to yourself. You must feel comfortable in how you present yourself to the wedding guests.
- Keep your shoulders and arms covered during the ceremony – with a shrug, stole, jacket or bolero, which can be taken off in the evening should you wish to bare your arms and shoulders then.
- Remember – the dress may be just for the day, but the photographs will last for ever!

Simon,

My 84-year-old mum is a loyal churchgoer, but
has come across a question that none of her clergy
can answer. God created Adam and Eve, who
had two sons, Cain and Abel. The Bible says
that Cain killed Abel and then took a wife. My
question is . . . where did the wife come from?

JANE in Newport Pagnell

REV. GRAHAM
Author and former vicar

Adam and Eve were just one of many tribes created
at the start of humanity. So it's very possible that
Cain married a woman from another tribe with a
completely different lineage.

> Hi Simon,
>
> After watching the football last night and hearing the commentators discussing the six-yard box, I asked my partner why it's referred to as 'the six-yard box' when the Europeans use metric measurements.
>
> He didn't know the answer, so we were wondering if any of your listeners could help.
>
> **ALI** in Dumfries

TOM in Preston
Former referee, now a referee assessor

The six-yard box is more commonly known as the 'goal area' according to guidelines set out by FIFA. The expression 'six-yard box' is just a British colloquialism – people everywhere else call it the 'goal area' in their own language.

Hello Simon and the team,

Can you tell me when Humpty Dumpty became an egg? In the nursery rhyme, there's no mention of what he/she/it is!

Perhaps someone out there might be able to explain where this comes from.

ADAM

RACHEL
Battle re-enactment society member

It is often thought that the nursery rhyme is a riddle, and an 'egg' is the answer. It's something that cannot be put back together once broken. Other layers of meaning are possible too. It could be a 'who am I?' riddle, and the answer might be Richard III, defeated at Bosworth Field in 1485 – so the nursery rhyme could have been a disguised way of poking fun at him. Or it might refer to a large cannon dislodged by Parliamentarians at the siege of Colchester in 1648. But the only 'egg' connection that makes sense is in the answer to a simple riddle.

Simon,

I have a 'social studies' sort of question. My great aunt, Florrie Walker, will be 107 on Saturday. Where does this put her in the league status of oldest woman/person in the world?

JOHN from Huddersfield

ROGER

At the time of writing, Besse Cooper is the oldest living person in the world, born 26 August 1891. She has four children, twelve grandchildren, fifteen great-grandchildren and one great-great-grandchild. Based on information found here: www.oldestinbritain.webs.com, Florrie Walker is probably ranked around 71 in the world . . .

> Simon,
>
> How was it decided which side of the road we should drive on?
>
> **MOLLY** in Kidderminster

BRIAN from Harrogate
'I just know!'

Horse-riders and carriage-drivers had their swords on the right, which meant they could draw them more easily when approaching a foe. Therefore, they would want to drive/ride on the left so that those coming towards them would pass on their right. Napoleon was left-handed, so he changed it on the continent in the countries he invaded.

‘IS THERE A
CONNECTION BETWEEN
THUNDERSTORMS
AND HEADACHES?’

Biological Brainteasers

Simon,

Why do the hairs on the back of my neck stand up when I hear a fantastic song or see something beautiful? I'm certainly not cold!

Thanks!

SAMANTHA in Eastbourne

DR SPINKS from Medway
GP

The hair follicles have tiny muscles attached to them, which contract when you're emotional due to the release of hormones and adrenaline. This makes the hairs on the back of your neck stand up.

Simon,

While watching the 100-metre final during the World Athletics Championship, I thought back to a time when the world record was around the 11-second mark – now a time of just over 9 seconds is normal.

My question: is there a point at which it would be physically impossible for a human to run 100 metres any faster?

HELEN in East Ilsley

PROFESSOR WILSON
From the Structure and Motion Lab, Royal Veterinary College

Obviously, there's a law of diminishing returns, but we have no reason to suppose that we won't continue to run faster and break records – as nutrition, training and human size and strength improve.

> Simon,
>
> *The other day, my daughter Freya asked me,*
> *'Why do we have fingerprints?'*
>   *I haven't a clue – maybe someone could help?*
>
> **SIMON** in Pontefract

JIM from Gourock
Crime scene examiner

We have fingerprints, also known as friction ridges, so we don't drop things. If we didn't have them, anything remotely slippery would fall through our fingers!

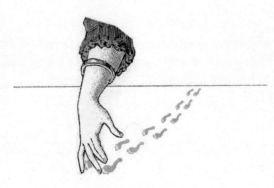

Simon,

We're all taught at a very early age that pillar-boxes are 'red', the sky is 'blue' and grass is 'green' – but how do we know that the green grass one person sees is the same colour that somebody else sees?

MARK in *Southend-on-Sea*

PHILIP in London
Author of Bright Earth: The Invention of Colour

It's a philosophical question. We know that everyone sees the same light, because we know the frequency of light. What we don't know is how brains interpret those frequencies. There's no reason why they shouldn't interpret them the same, but we can't be sure.

Simon,

I recently went to a wedding and was delighted to see four of my favourite hymns on the order of service. However, I couldn't help noticing that most of the guests were struggling to hit the high notes.

Is there any evidence that the pitch of the average human voice has dropped since these hymns were written? Have our lungs and larynxes grown bigger?

KATE in Baldock

TIM from Winchester
Mature student studying the voice; also member of the British Voice Association

There has been no real change physiologically, this is just about a lack of practice. You wouldn't expect Fred Bloggs to enter an athletics championship without any training, and it's the same with the voice. The problem is that women's natural voices are actually lower than we think, and decrease in pitch as they age, so that singing in a higher register needs practice in both singing and breathing. It's always been the case, according to the experts, that unpractised congregations struggle with the hymns. This may also be exacerbated by whatever hymnal is in use, since some pitch the hymns quite high – the BBC's *Songs of Praise* is notorious for this!

Simon,

I recently had to confiscate an A4 portfolio wallet from a colleague because the noise of her scratching the textured material was too much for me to bear.

Why is it that when someone scrapes a blackboard with a fingernail, or drags a knife along a plate or a chair across a hard floor, many of us cringe and howl in displeasure at the noise?

PAUL in Swindon

ANDREW
British Society of Audiology

It's the high frequencies (typically between 2,000 and 4,000 kHz), coupled with the roughness and sharpness of the sounds, which make them unpleasant to the ear.

> Simon,
>
> When I was in my twenties, I used to go out, drink copious amounts of alcohol, flop into bed in a drunken haze, and usually wake up ready to do battle with the day ahead with no significant side-effects.
>
> Now that I'm in my early forties, I can't drink half the quantity I used to, and I wake up with a monumental hangover that takes days to get over!
>
> What has changed that I can no longer process the alcohol?
>
> **SAMANTHA** in Eastbourne

DR GERRY from Trowbridge
Former university lecturer and head of medicine management

 The changes are down to two main factors:

1. The alteration in the ratio of body water and fat: the proportion of water decreases with age, so a given quantity of alcohol will result in higher levels (of alcohol) in the blood of an older person.

2. The liver's ability to detoxify alcohol diminishes with age. Consequently the rate of removal of alcohol from the body slows down.

Please drink responsibly!

Simon,

Why do we get butterflies in the stomach, and what are they? Going over hump-backed bridges and going too high on swings causes them, but strong emotions do as well – why?

TONI in Northern Ireland

DR OVAISE from Bristol
Consultant psychiatrist

It is a primitive fight-or-flight response. Fear, excitement and the resulting adrenaline divert blood away from the organs, including the stomach, towards the muscles. In combination with the increased heart-rate, this creates the butterfly sensation.

Simon,

Every time the 'Mayo! Simon May-a-ayo!' jingle is on, I always seem to sing along perfectly in tune. Does this mean I have perfect pitch, or is it familiarity through repetition?
What makes a person pitch perfect?

WILLIAM in Scotland

JUNE from Nether Kellet
Head of music at grammar school

There is no such thing as perfect pitch – only memory pitch . . . Either way, it's the ability to hit any note exactly without an external cue – so it wouldn't apply in your case because you are using the jingle.

> Simon,
>
> *I've just eaten some mints and my mouth has gone cold, and so has my breath. I've always wondered, why does that happen?*
>
> **EMILY**, aged 14

KENNETH from Glasgow
Chemistry teacher

Mints are made with oil from the mint plant, which contains a chemical called menthol. When you consume a mint, the oil dissolves and creates a cooling sensation inside your mouth. Your mouth feels cold, but it hasn't actually gone cold. It's a little chemical trick performed by the menthol on the chill receptors in your mouth and skin.

Dear Simon,

I know we get it from our parents' genes, but why exactly are our eyes brown, blue, grey or green? And is it true that people with blue eyes withstand the cold better?

Hope you can help!

FRANCESCA, aged 8, in Bradford

ELLIE from Bromsgrove
GCSE biology student – got an A* for a recent project on this!

In our DNA there are instructions on how to make different enzymes. The enzymes control reactions in cells. These reactions create colours, or pigments. It is said that brown pigment, from an evolutionary point of view, shields your eyes better in the sunlight.

The reason there are only some colours is because some genes are stronger than others – brown is the strongest, while blue is the weakest. Whichever of your parents has the strongest gene, that is the one you will most likely get.

One theory states that blue eyes arose due to a single genetic mutation in response to the cold weather of Northern Europe, as lighter eyes are better able to see in these conditions. However, this isn't generally accepted so it's quite likely that people with blue eyes are no better able to withstand the cold that those with brown eyes.

Simon, can you help?

If the average human brain was to be replaced by a computer with a processing power to conduct all bodily functions (i.e. seeing, hearing, talking, moving, thinking, eating, etc.), what would be the equivalent processor speed, hard-drive capacity, RAM and cache memory required in order to function properly?

Thanks!

BRUCE in Huddersfield

DAN from London
Neuroscientist

Using the most powerful computer in the world, a chap called Henry Markram managed to simulate one neuron in the brain of a rat. There are probably about a billion of those. In the human brain it is estimated there are 90 billion neurons – you get the idea . . .

> Simon,
>
> I recently spent a day walking around London, but ended up in agony as my feet were killing me. I want to take part in a 10-kilometre race soon but that will be further agony.
>
> I am sure that loads of your listeners will be marathon runners and can advise me about how to prepare my feet for this – should the skin on the soles of my feet be hard or soft, and should I run with or without socks?
>
> **MARION** in Bury St Edmunds

JIMMY from Lincolnshire
Retired runner – ran 120 marathons, all over the world

 You need to make sure you are wearing the correct, well-cushioned shoes. Always wear socks because they soak up the sweat! Clean feet regularly to keep them healthy. Before running, rub Vaseline in between the toes.

Simon,

When I sneeze, it's a straightforward normal sneeze. However, when I was pregnant with my son, this changed to two sneezes in quick succession. Why did this happen, and is double sneezing common for pregnant women?

Thanks!

CAROLINE in Farringdon

ANDREW
President of the British Rhinological Society

 This is not something I'm familiar with personally, but a physiological explanation would be that in pregnancy there's a hormonal change, which could lead to greater nose congestion and sensitivity, and therefore perhaps to double sneezing.

Simon,

As a family we are always late, no matter how organized I try to be. My father was always late, and I have married a 'late' man – we were both even late to our wedding!

Why is it some people are always on time, and some are always late? Could it be something genetic that makes us perceive time differently, or is it purely that we are disorganized, and it's a learnt behaviour?

ANNABEL and family in Suffolk

NICOLA from Welwyn Garden City
Personal performance coach

 I'd say this stems from three things, none of them genetics:

1) **Expectations**
   You have created an expectation that you will always be late. It would take away the fun of family gatherings and so on if you were to start turning up on time. You'd no longer be the focal point.

2) **Beliefs**
   You do not believe you can be on time. You believe you will always be late and, in order to validate your own beliefs, you always are.

3) **Motivation**
   Being on time is not something that is important to you. If punctuality was high on your list of values, you would be on time. I bet if I offered your family £3 million to meet me somewhere at a given time, you'd make very certain you got there on time!

Simon,

I've been playing netball for a number of years. At 5ft 9in, I'm invariably put in defence, but I don't seem to jump as high as most of my team. Are people born springy, or is there a group of muscles I can train to make me jump higher?

Or is it just because my brain is lazy and thinks that because I'm tall, I'll reach the ball anyway?

ELAINE in Woking

MIKE from Perth
Elite athlete coach

If you can't jump high enough, it's because you lack type 2B muscles; you probably have more type 1 muscles. You can build type 2B up using the correct training – and then you'll be able to jump higher.

Hi Simon,

The other day I had a really bad headache. I went home ready for bed, but then a thunderstorm broke and within an hour my headache had gone. So I wondered – is there a connection between thunderstorms and headaches?

Any help would be appreciated!

JULIE in Macclesfield

PAUL from Bridgend
Electronics engineer, studied physics at university

Static charge builds up on the clouds before a thunderstorm. As our brain operates using electrical impulses, many people are affected by the increased charge in the atmosphere, giving them a headache. When the storm breaks, the charge disappears (and so does the headache).

Simon,

My 8-year-old son Tom asked me today, while we were in the car, why it was that when he's lying in bed and it's quiet, he can still hear a 'silent noise'.
   I told him to ask his dad later, but I thought it would be a good homework question.

DEBBIE in Old Basing

DR SPINKS from Medway
GP

The carotid and facial arteries run very close to the ear. You can hear the blood flowing through them when it is completely quiet. Normally, the brain is good at ignoring noises, but paradoxically it's more difficult to ignore this noise when it is silent elsewhere.

Please can you help me with my biology homework?

Why do your fingernails grow quicker than your toenails? And while we're at it – why does the hair on your head grow faster than the hair elsewhere on your body?

Thanks, Simon!

CLARE

DR SAHOTA from London
Consultant dermatologist

Nails grow from something called the nail matrix. When you are young, they grow flat. As you get older, toenails grow slightly upwards, and also thicker, which means they grow more slowly. The fact that toenails are thicker than fingernails probably also explains why they grow more slowly, whatever age you are. Better diets today mean that our nails grow faster than those of our grandparents' generation.

The hair on your arms stays shorter because its cells are programmed to stop growing every couple of months. In contrast, the hair on your head can grow very long because the follicles are programmed to let hair grow for years at a time.

> Simon,
>
> Why do we get headaches in certain parts of our brain, for example behind the eyes, or the back of the head?
>
> **JOSH** in Sheffield

TIM from Alton
Osteopath

The ones at the front tend to be caused by the eyes (eyestrain, etc.), and the ones at the back tend to be muscular problems, relating to the neck and so on. Likewise, a headache behind one eye is usually a cluster headache or a migraine. Because there are different muscles in our head, we notice and feel headaches in different parts of our head.

My *daughter Kirsty, aged 11, likes the odd piece of chewing gum. We – Mum and Dad – have told her that you should always put gum in the bin when you've finished with it. She would like to know why you can't swallow gum. Does it do something to your tummy if you swallow it?*

WILMA in Coatbridge

EVELYN in London
Dietician

A small amount doesn't do you any harm, it just passes through the system – but it's dangerous to swallow large amounts because it could get attached to other things you consume and block the digestive tract. It's rubber, which is why it doesn't get broken down.

Simon,

I've just come back from the Goodwood Festival of Speed and noticed that I have more earwax than normal. This leads me to think that my ears have produced more wax to protect themselves from the ridiculous amount of noise they've been subjected to over the weekend.

Is that what earwax is for, or does it have another purpose?

SIMON in Preston

MIKE from Stone
Hearing-aid audiologist

Earwax has three uses. It's a moisturizer for the skin in the ear canal, preventing itchy, dry ears, it's sticky to catch dirt and debris, and it's acidic so it kills bacteria. There are various reasons why we sometimes suffer a build up of earwax, and constant exposure to very loud noise is among them.

Simon,

If we wash our hands using soap with cold water, does that adequately do the job? Or is it essential to have warm water to make sure our hands are really clean?

RICHARD in Newcastle upon Tyne

ALAN from Huddersfield
Ambulance service vehicle cleaner

It used to be more about the heat of the water, because hot water killed more bacteria. Now soaps are antibacterial, so it's more about the length of time you wash your hands for, with the heat of the water being just about comfort. We're told 1½–2 minutes is about right.

Simon,

I remember one summer day as a child, a friend and I spent the whole afternoon banging our funny bones against a stone post to see who could get the biggest tingle in their arm. I'm not sure who won, but we both ended up with numb arms.

My question is, what is the funny bone and what's the point of it? Can we place it in the same useless bracket as the appendix?

MATT *in* Walsall

DANNY
Associate professor of physiology

It's the ulnar nerve, which runs from your neck, down your upper arm and through the joint in your elbow. When you hit your elbow at a particular angle, you bang the nerve, sending shockwaves through your lower arm to your hand, hence 'pins and needles'. The nerves at the elbow are rather exposed, which is probably why it happens.

> Simon,
>
> *I'm a teacher and I always feel sorry for students who go bright red when they are asked to speak in front of the class. They are already nervous and embarrassed and getting a red face only draws attention to that.*
>
> *Is there a scientific, biological explanation as to why we blush?*
>
> **FIONA** in Coventry

TREVOR
Consultant surgeon with an interest in the treatment of blushing

There is no known evolutionary purpose for blushing, though it was once thought that blushing was a sign of affection. Equally, nobody knows why some people blush more than others. Northern Europeans tend to have a particular problem – with particularly high cases of blushing recorded in Scandinavia.

Simon,

During the school Christmas hols, our 9-year-old daughter got into some pretty bad habits when it came to getting to bed on time. When her mum told her she'd get bags under her eyes, my daughter asked, 'Why do you get bags under your eyes, and why do they call them bags?'

DAVID in Devon

DR LOWE from London
Consultant dermatologist

The area of skin under the eyes is thin, and it easily shows the effects of tiredness. Under-eye bags are called bags because they get filled up! The dark circles under your eyes are caused by sluggish blood flow. Rubbing your eyes, which inflames the area, releasing darker blood vessels, can also be a cause. Facial skin pigment can also contribute towards dark circles under your eyes.

> *Dear Simon and team,*
>
> *My young grandson clutched his side after racing around the park recently, and I told him he had a 'stitch'. This got me wondering – what exactly is a stitch? And what causes pain in your side when you run?*
>
> ## JACQUI

JOHN from Chesham
Professor of sports science

A stitch is a spasm in the diaphragm, the muscle that separates the chest, where the heart and lungs are, from the abdomen. There are various theories, but the most likely is that stitches are caused by lack of oxygen to the muscle fibres in the diaphragm. Good posture and breathing techniques help prevent stitch. Children tend to get them more than adults; in other words, it's something we can grow out of.

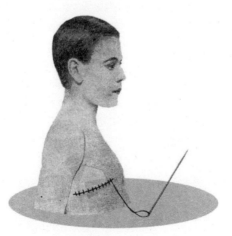

> Simon,
>
> A problem I have been pondering for the last couple of years – since it started happening to me, basically – is why is my beard grey/white, when my hair – which has been with me a lot longer – is still very dark brown?
>
> **ANDREW** in Peterborough

JERRY from Harrogate
Hairdresser of 36 years' experience

 There is no guarantee that your beard will go grey before the rest of your hair. It could equally be the other way round. It depends on your genetic make-up, and on when different parts of your body stop producing melanin – the stuff that colours your hair.

> Dear Simon,
>
> We all know it's possible to cough in our sleep, but is it possible to sneeze when sleeping? Obviously, sneezing is involuntary, but does the body stop us doing it overnight?
>
> Also, if this is the case, can our noses still drip while we're asleep? Perhaps one of your listeners in the medical profession could help me out!
>
> **ANDREW** in West Yorkshire

SARAH
Radio 2's very own doctor

 You can sneeze in your sleep, even though you might wake yourself up! As for runny noses, because you're lying down, the mucus tends to go backwards rather than dripping from your nose. Coughs get worse overnight, however.

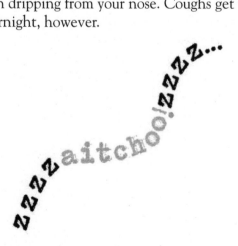

Hello Simon and the team,

I have a question about blood. When we lick our blood, like if we have a cut on our finger or arm or something, does that blood go back into your body as blood? Or is it broken down?

FLO, aged 10

RACHEL from Usk
Nurse

 Blood – which is rich in minerals – is broken down in your digestive system, with the good bits recycled.

Simon,

While on holiday recently, our 4-year-old son Archie came out with a question that I couldn't answer either with the truth or with any other theory that you can get away with while they're still this little . . .

The question was: what is skin made of?

CASIE in Peterborough

GAIL from Edinburgh
Skin therapist

Skin is made up of five layers with all sorts of things in it, such as fat, blood vessels and hair follicles, but the top layer is predominantly a protein called keratin, which is what your hair and nails are also made of.

Simon,

*I'm hurtling towards sixty, but still have a good
head of hair – white though, and beginning to thin
on top. However, I'm now finding the equivalent
of a rainforest growing out of my nose, ears and
eyebrows.*

Why does this happen when you get older?

NIGEL in Sutton-in-Craven

JOHN from Edinburgh
Pathologist

It's a hormonal shift in males, with testosterone levels
falling and oestrogen levels rising . . . This new
growth of hair is unfortunately a normal part of male
ageing. No one is entirely sure what makes it happen,
but one theory is that as you age, the hair follicles
in and around your ears and nose may become more
sensitive to the male hormone testosterone, which
stimulates the unwanted hair growth.

The other day my son Ben, aged 3, had hiccups. Naturally enough he asked me why he was hiccuping.

I'm a doctor and I had no answer – please help me!!

ED in Taunton

DR MOSLEY from Dunoon
GP

Hiccups result from an irritation of the diaphragm, which causes it to spasm involuntarily. The diaphragm plays a part in breathing, and when it spasms, it makes you breathe in very quickly. The sudden inward rush of air gets stopped in the throat, which creates the 'hic' sound.

'WHY DO WE HAVE TO PUT "U" AFTER "Q"?'

Literature and Language

Simon,

Can an animal from the UK communicate with an animal of its own species anywhere in the world as easily as it can communicate with a local own species? Or are there regional differences in their 'language'?

STEPHEN

DR ROBINSON
Lectures on the evolution of language

Animals don't speak different 'languages' from country to country, but there are recognized differences in their accents. This has been observed in chimpanzees, is noticeable in birdsong across the UK, and can even be heard in dog barks.

Simon,

Who wrote the first autobiography?

KIM in Retford

PHILIP
Postgrad theology student

The first proper autobiography came in the
fourth century AD, in the form of St Augustine's
'Confessions', written in what is now Tunisia, where
he tells of his life as a young man before his famous
conversion to being a monk.

> Simon,
>
> In languages like French or Spanish, how is the gender of different objects decided?
> For example, why is a table female in both those languages?
>
> **KATY** in Hatfield Broad Oak

PROFESSOR CRYSTAL
One of the country's foremost professors of linguistics

There are no rules! Way back, centuries ago, when modern languages were forming, then there was some order to it, but nowadays it is arbitrary, and in many cases dependent on how the words sound.

> Simon,
>
> I've been set a homework assignment to memorize some Spanish verbs. Please could you suggest an easy and successful way of remembering them?
>
> Thanks!
>
> **FREYA**, aged 11, in Plymouth

JO from Bilsthorpe
Spanish teacher

Spanish regular verbs fall into three main groups: ending in -ar, -er or -ir. The Spanish language tends not to use pronouns (I, you, he, she, etc.) so, for example, just one word will mean 'I eat'. The key to success therefore is to recognize and learn the appropriate endings for each person, add them to the verb's stem and, woo hoo, you can grapple with most regular Spanish verbs!

Simon,

My son's class is doing poetry and he asked me what makes a good poem.

I, of course, have no idea – but could you and your team help perhaps?

BELINDA in Surrey

LISA from Leamington Spa
English teacher

A good poem is what has often been thought but never so well expressed. (With thanks to Alexander Pope, eighteenth-century English poet.)

Simon,

Do snakes have a language?

CATRINA in Huntington

COLIN from Driffield
Amateur herpetologist

 Snakes don't have ears, they are deaf. They find mates and hunt using smells, which they detect through their tongues.

Simon,

I have asked this question of many people, but no one has come up with a decent answer. This is where your show comes in. I am hoping you might explain why you have to put a 'U' after every 'Q' in English. There is no word in the English language that does not follow this rule. Surely, if it's there all the time, it might as well not be there any of the time? Think of the money we'd save in ink!

TOBY in Brighton

JOHN
Emeritus professor of English language and cultural tradition

 It's an anomaly from the Middle Ages, when contemporary language was being formed. We could change it tomorrow if we wanted, but it's become linguistically ingrained.

Simon,

My question is about surnames – when and where did they start and why have they finished? Surely all the Smiths, Wrights, Archers, etc. must have had names before they had a trade? And why has no one invented any new names – why no Mr Dustman, Mr Fireman or Mr Manager, though no doubt there's a Mr and Mrs Webb-Paige somewhere . . .

Any light shed on this would be much appreciated!

ANDREW in Dorset

ROB in Doncaster
Genealogist

Surnames came about when the poll tax was taken in the twelfth century, to distinguish between different people in the same village with the same forename. New surnames still appear occasionally now but they no longer are job- or village-related.

> Simon,
>
> My nephew has been asked to make his language choices for his third year at senior school. He must choose between Russian and Japanese. Can anyone help him make the right decision please? What is considered the best language to learn?
>
> Many thanks!
>
> ### LAURA in Birmingham

CLAIRE from Birmingham

Teaches English as a foreign language and studies languages and cognitive linguistics

I'd recommend that your nephew should take Japanese, as it will be a good way to expand his knowledge of language systems beyond (what I presume has been) a largely European sphere. Knowledge of a wide variety of language grammars and cultures is proven to be extremely beneficial, as it expands a person's cognitive perceptions of world phenomena and tends to produce people who are cleverer than those who are monolingual. I learned some Japanese in senior school and it has greatly helped me to learn both Chinese and Korean later in life, as some of the basic grammar patterns were already laid down. *Seikou wo inorimasu!*

'HOW SOON AFTER EATING CAKE DO WE PUT ON WEIGHT?'

Home Economics for Grown-ups

> *Simon,*
>
> *If you were only able to eat one or two meals for the rest of your life, what would be the best choice to give you the full range of nutrients you need to stay fit and healthy?*
>
> **CLARE** in Derbyshire

HUGH from Birdlip
Chef

 Fish (for protein), steamed vegetables (steaming keeps more nutrients in), rice (for carbs) and coconut sauce – in fact, you can virtually live off coconuts alone since they have everything you need to survive.

Simon,

Does my dog appreciate me buying him a variety of dog food flavours, or would the same flavour every day do?

JULIA

SHARON from Ilminster
Vet

Dogs have taste buds and can distinguish flavour, and they have taste memory. Hence they may appear fussy. However, if you don't indulge this fussiness, they will eat anything. They don't have a complicated relationship with food like humans do.

Simon,

How does the Queen decide what to have for tea every day? Does she have a set menu? How far in advance does she decide – and what if she just fancies a 'chippie tea' or pizza?

GARETH in Northampton

PENNY JUNOR from Malmesbury
Royal biographer

The Queen is likely to sit down with her chef and decide on her meals on a daily basis. She doesn't like spicy or garlicky foods. She prefers simple food, with quite a plain taste.

At state dinners, she – and probably most heads of state – will avoid messy foods such as spaghetti, so as not to get spots on her clothes.

Simon,

It's peak broad-bean season in my vegetable garden. Why do bright green beans leave the water below a rich red colour when steamed? Have I lost all the valuable good vitamins?

SIMON in Hinton Charterhouse

KAREN from York
Grows her own vegetables

The iron in the chlorophyll, which gives the beans their green colour, turns red when it's oxidized through the steaming process – in the same way as metal rusts when it's oxidized.

Simon,

I recently bought my usual brand of Cheddar from a well-known supermarket, only to discover it was orange in colour instead of yellow. Why are some cheeses different colours? Is there a colouring process involved?

PAUL in Monmouthshire

CAROL from Bristol

Works as a technical manager for a farmhouse cheese-maker

All cheeses start off looking exactly the same. Maturity and the time of year can alter the shade slightly. However, big differences in colour are down to a colouring process – you're right.

Hi, Simon,

After drinking a can of a well-known brand of cola this afternoon, a thought occurred to me – this would taste much better from a glass bottle . . .

Why is it that cola, milk and sauces such as ketchup taste better from a glass bottle than from cans or plastic bottles?

JOSH in Walsall

TIM from Hitchen
Used to work in the drinks industry

Glass is non-permeable, while aluminium and plastic are semi-permeable, which means there is some loss of gas and oxygen, and hence the slight difference in taste.

> Simon,
>
> Why do so many ice-cream vans play the tune 'Greensleeves'?
>
> **STEVE** in Sheffield

PAUL from Ascot
Musician

It has no official composer – although Henry VIII is rumoured to have written it – and is out of copyright, so they don't have to pay any money to PRS (the Performing Right Society) when they play it.

Simon,

Many foods and cosmetics have added vitamins, e.g. vitamin A or vitamin C – but I would like to know what a vitamin looks like.

How do we know what to look for, when wanting to isolate a vitamin?

TONY in Reading

SARAH from Bishop's Stortford
Degree in biochemistry

Vitamins were initially thought to belong to the amine family, all of which contain nitrogen ('vital amines', hence the name), though this has since been disproved. They do all, however, contain carbon, and this helps to identify them.

You can cultivate vitamins in a laboratory, hence the ability to 'add' them to foods and cosmetics.

> Simon,
>
> If I eat ten cream cakes, when will I gain the weight? Is it a matter of minutes, hours or days?
>
> ### KAY in Newcastle-under-Lyme

RUTH from London
Registered dietician

 If you eat five cakes (say, 1000 calories over the recommended daily allowance) one day, but are otherwise healthy, the weight gain will be negligible. However, if you did this every day, you would put on two pounds in seven days – and long-term there would be other health issues too.

Simon,

For reasons I won't bore you with, I managed to leave curry sauce on an unpeeled banana. I want to use the banana to make a cake. My daughter says I shouldn't because it will have absorbed the flavour and smell of the curry. What I want to know is how tastes and smells transfer between foods. And does this apply to my banana, given that it is still in the skin, and therefore protected from the sauce?

JANET in Rothwell

GERARD from Roos
Chef and food biologist

Foods and other things you smell are molecules that have been naturally shed. When you smell something, it is the olfactory receptors in your nose picking up the molecules in the air. Just as the molecules bind to the receptors in your nose, so can they attach themselves to, and be absorbed by, other things. Hence the transference of smell and flavour.

Simon,

I've just had a banana for lunch, and it struck me how many miles this has travelled, and the cost involved. How much would bananas cost if we could grow them in our climate, and they were therefore delivered locally?

NICK *in* Yeovil

TERRY from the Rhondda Valley
Jeremy Vine's resident agricultural expert

The cost would decrease greatly, as you'd save a huge amount on travel costs. Farming bananas is not labour-intensive, so the amount of extra money spent on labour wouldn't cancel out the amount saved on transport.

Simon,

Why is it that mayonnaise is weighed in grams and not in millilitres? Is it not a liquid? How is it decided which units of measurement to use?
(From the Drivetime *fridge: HP sauce is in grams, ketchup is in both.)*

HARRY, aged 13

VIC from Oxford
Professor of biogeochemistry

We can measure things in mass or volume. Things that can be poured tend to get measured by volume, and things that can't, by mass. In the case of your ketchup/mayo, the decision would have been arbitrary. We used to measure peas by volume, for instance, and in America they use cups as a measure for ingredients like sugar and flour when cooking.

Dear Simon,

I am struggling with a dilemma in our household.

   I have two children – 18 and 15, boy and girl. I frequently fill our fridge with what I consider to be exciting, nutritious options, both sweet and savoury. However, when either of my teenagers opens the fridge, they just look longingly into it, sigh and shut the door.

   What do they want to find there?

LINDA in Kenilworth

HEATHER from Orpington
Teenager

Mountain Dew, cans of fizzy drink, lots of cheese, yoghurts, ham (eaten straight from the packet), lots of milk . . . basically food that requires no preparation!

NATHALIE in Woking
Mother of three, two of them teenagers

Pastries, sausage rolls, 'Cheese Strings', ham (eaten straight out of the packet).

   My children will cook eggs and bacon, though.

Dear Simon,

What is the purpose of the sense of taste? Surely it can only be damaging to us when we like the taste of things that are bad for us? Is this an evolutionary mistake, or is there a purpose behind it?

ALICE in Haslemere

GERARD from Roos
Food historian and trained evolutionary biologist

Things that are dangerous taste bitter. That's why we developed taste. Things we like tend to be quite rare in nature, but we have managed to make them very available to us via supermarkets and so on, which is where the danger lies.

Simon,

On the way home from school, my mum and I were tucking into one of those well-known segmented orange-flavoured spheres.

This one had the added wonder of popping candy inside, so I wondered who invented popping candy, and how does it start to pop when you swallow it?

SOPHIE in Hampshire

DAWN from Chichester
Runs a chocolaterie

Popping candy is made with sugar, glucose syrup, lactose and carbon dioxide, as well as flavouring and colouring. It was patented by General Foods; their research chemist William A. Mitchell was trying to make an instant soft drink when he discovered it.

Simon,

My 18-month-old boy Lucas received a bottle of whisky as a christening present. The friend who bought it suggested we keep it until Lucas's eighteenth, so he can have it as his first legal drink.

My question is, what is the best way to store it? Should I keep it somewhere warm or cold, lay it down or stand it up?

Your help would be much appreciated!

MARK in Horndean

MARTIN in Edinburgh
Whisky specialist

The whisky should be stored upright, to prevent damage to the cork. It should be stored at an even temperature, out of direct sunlight. Whisky itself doesn't age once it's left the barrel, so it will remain the same age as it is now, as long as it remains sealed.

> Simon,
>
> I am planning on making a Christmas wreath this year and I want to include sprouts in the greenery. I know this might not be everyone's idea of a Christmas delight, but it will make me smile.
>
> My question is – is there any way of preserving fresh sprouts so they don't start to go brown and smelly while hanging on my front door!
>
> **TESSA** *in Kent*

ALISON
Florist in Moreton-in-Marsh

 You need to wire them and spray them with something called leaf shine, which we florists use. This should preserve them for four weeks, which will see you to Xmas.

Simon,

While clearing out my cupboards to make way for Christmas fayre, I found some assorted herbal teabags dating back to 1997! Should I throw them out? How long does herbal tea keep for?

CHRISTINE in Taunton

ALISON from Market Drayton
Herbalist

Herbal tea-wise: anything still in its packet or sealed, use before the best-before date. Anything loose should be used within a year.

> Simon,
>
> Can anybody identify what it is about Brussels sprouts that makes them unpalatable to a large section of the population?
>
> And is there any way to make sprouts nicer to eat that I haven't tried already? (I've tried boiling, frying, steaming, roasting, serving with chicken, with bacon, with other veg, finely chopped, very fresh, etc., etc.)
>
> **KAY** in Muir of Ord

ZOE
Spokesperson for the Institute of Food Research

It's a chemical called sinigrin that gives the sprout its bitter taste. It's found in cabbage and broccoli too. It helps protect the plant from pests. I guess if you don't like it, you don't like it!

Simon,

When cooking with alcohol, how much of it burns off during cooking? Does it depend on the temperature reached?

At this festive time, I don't want to put anyone over the drink-drive limit with the food . . . !

KATH in Doncaster

MARK from Peterborough
Keen cook and amateur scientist

Alcohol boils at around 78°C, so as soon as you get beyond that point, it will start to burn off. The key thing, of course, is *not* to boil mulled wine – so you shouldn't drive having drunk it. Alcohol on your pud will probably still be there because the pudding will be served below 78 degrees.

> Simon,
>
> How are flavourings made?
>
> **JENKY**

OLLY from Bath
A-level chemistry student

Flavourings are generally carbon-based compounds, particularly smells. Fruit flavourings, for example, are often a type of compound called an ester. This is made by reacting an alcohol (not necessarily ethanol) with a carboxylic acid (for instance vinegar, or the formic acid made by ants).

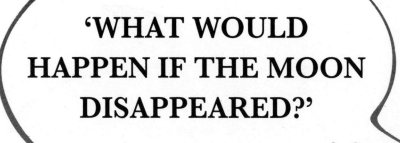

'WHAT WOULD
HAPPEN IF THE MOON
DISAPPEARED?'

*The Weird and
Wonderful World*

Simon,

Which are the five fastest aeroplanes in the world?
I need to know for my flight project at school!

NOAH, aged 10

IAN from Heathrow
Airline pilot

 Here they are:

1. Space Shuttle
2. X-15
3. Valkyrie XB-70
4. SR-71 (aka YF-12A)
5. MiG-25

The fastest passenger aircraft is the TU-144.

Simon,

Having watched Wallace & Gromit's A Grand Day Out, my son Samuel (aged 3) would now like to know how much a rocket would cost that could take him to the moon.

Thank you,

FIONA in Inkpen

HEATHER
Astronomer and space expert

A billion pounds all in – from construction, to all the people involved in building and launching, to the launch and fuel costs.

Simon,

Why are there no photos or video material of the so-called 'dark side' of the moon?

When the moon passes between the earth and the sun, isn't the dark side of the moon in total daylight?

MIKE in Stockton

RICHARD from Devizes
RAF navigator, trained in celestial positioning

The moon does rotate on its own polar axis, but at exactly the same rate that it revolves around the earth, thus always presenting one face to us on earth.

Until the space age the other side was known as the dark side because no human had ever seen it, but it was not literally dark because the sun illuminates all of the moon once per lunar day (on average every 28 earth days). It has in fact now been mapped and photographed, so pictures do exist.

> *Dear Simon,*
>
> *Having sailed for a number of years, I have some basic knowledge of meteorology.*
>
> *We know that when the isobars are close together the wind is stronger, but no one's been able to explain to me – simply – what causes it to gust.*
>
> *Help!*
>
> **MIKE** in Bedford

NEIL from East Brent
Sailor and amateur meteorologist

Wind speed varies with altitude – the higher up you go, the faster the wind blows. On settled days there is not much vertical movement between the layers in the atmosphere so you feel a constant wind speed at whatever height you are, with the lowest at ground level and increasing as you go up.

When things get more unsettled, with storm clouds and thunderstorms and so on, there is a lot of *vertical* movement in the air, and these smooth layers get disturbed – warm air rises up due to convection and cold air gets forced down.

And that's what a gust is – air (usually colder) from high up and therefore moving faster, being forced down to a lower altitude (and eventually ground level) by the vertical movement of turbulent air caused by convection.

> *Simon,*
>
> *People are always talking about what would happen to our planet if the sun disappeared – but I would like to know what would happen if the moon disappeared?*
>
> **HARRY** in Leiston

STEPHEN in Frome
Has an O-level in astronomy

The lack of moon would affect not only the tides, but also the atmosphere, which would in turn wreak havoc on our climate, and be catastrophic to life on earth.

On top of this, we would have lost our main defence against incoming asteroids, and be more susceptible to these crashing down to earth.

END OF THE WORLD, basically.

Dear Simon,

After our chemistry class proved that water cannot ever get hotter than 100° Celsius, clever Katie asked: 'If we got a titanium container, filled it to the brim, sealed the container so it was completely water-tight, and then heated the container until the titanium was near its melting point, would the water inside get hotter than 100 degrees C?'

Many thanks,

MRS BIRSE, Joe, Cameron, Hollie, Annabel, Marcus, Tamsin, Ava, Megan, Matt, Amber, Ella, Daniel, Peter and clever Katie (Year 5X at Meoncross School in Fareham)

STEVE from the Wirral
Science teacher

It absolutely can get hotter. All boiling is essentially turning something from liquid to gas. Stop it doing that and it will continue to heat up. It will heat until the titanium melts, at which point – get the heck out of there!!!

Dear Simon,

Inspired by the first episode of Bruce Parry's
Arctic on BBC2, in which he had a mountain
named after him, I started to wonder just how
much of the world remains unmapped? Can you
buy a paper map for everywhere?

VAL in Reading

ALAN in Brackley
From Global Mapping

Yes, the whole world is mapped, and paper maps are
available of everywhere. It just depends on the scale
you want.

Simon,

Why is it that some musical notes when put together sound awful, whereas others make a wonderful tune?

What is the science behind the formation of musical notes?

Thanks!

RICHARD in Rochdale

HUW in Chichester
Director of music at a secondary school

It's to do with the harmonic spectrum. Notes oscillate, and some oscillations correspond more closely than others. If the frequencies overlap or are very similar, the notes will sound good together. For the science behind it all, we'd need a lot more space and time!

> Hi Simon,
>
> I've often wondered – how do they get electricity into batteries? It's something that's puzzled me for a while and I'm hoping one of your listeners can help.
>
> Thanks!
>
> **THOMAS**, aged 10, in Guildford

JEREMY from Hilperton
Metallurgist

There are two dissimilar materials in the battery, along with an electrolyte (usually acid). These three things react against each other, with electrons flowing from one material to the other, thus creating a flow of electricity.

Don't ask about rechargeables as they are way too complicated!

Simon,

My son William came home from school one night having asked his chemistry teacher a question she couldn't answer. The teacher then asked the entire science department, and they had no clue either.

The question is: when cooking oil rubs on to a piece of paper, why does the paper become translucent?

Hope you can help!

JOHN in Plymouth

PAUL from Slough
Chemist

When anything is coated in oil it looks shiny, because it then reflects more light than it absorbs. The oil does the same thing to the structure of the paper: it coats all of the surfaces right through the sheet, making the fibres absorb less light. Less light absorbed means more light comes through, thus it appears translucent.

Simon,

As I was getting into my car one day after a thick frost, I saw the roof was covered in the most beautiful fern-like shapes. These ferns were arranged in a very uniform manner, being similar size and shape and oriented in the same direction, like a large paisley pattern.

Why does frost form these particular curved fern shapes? What controls the size, shape and orientation of the ferns?

BRIAN in Olney

CLIVE from Basingstoke
Knows about cars!

It's probably to do with the polish originally applied to the car's roof, and any polishing done subsequently. Unless it's completely even, which it hardly ever is, the frost follows the polish lines. Ice crystallization is also affected by other imperfections and dust, dirt and pollen – like the polish, these all contribute to the formation of beautiful shapes on the car roof's surface.

Simon,

I was watching Great Barrier Reef *on BBC2, and I was surprised to learn that only 7 per cent of the reef is coral.*

Can someone explain what makes up the other 93 per cent?

SIMON *in Grantham*

MONTY HALL
Presenter of Great Barrier Reef

I was just listening to the show and heard you ask about the excellent and informative series that was *Great Barrier Reef*! Well, to answer the question, the remaining 93 per cent is made up of a lagoon with an area one and a half times the size of Great Britain, 600 islands, and a spattering of mangrove swamps and fringing rainforests.

Simon,

The other night, my son and I were star-gazing and he asked me, 'How much does the moon weigh?'

I found I had no answer, as I considered that gravity is less on the moon and such technical things are far above my abilities.

Can you help?

EDDIE in Pittsburgh

DR WHITEHOUSE, near Farnborough
Astronomer and author of The Moon: A Biography

The best way to measure the mass of an object is to put something in orbit around it, like a satellite. Then, using Newton's Theory of Gravity, we can work out the mass of the object, which in this case is:
$$(7 \times 10^{22})\text{kg}$$
or: 70 thousand billion billion kilos!
This is approximately 1 per cent of the earth's mass.

Simon,

I seem to remember years ago the exciting scientific innovation of cloud 'seeding', which made it rain in parts of the world where it was very dry.

We have our fair share of clouds here even if it isn't raining, so would it be possible – in theory – to make it rain and alleviate any drought in the UK using cloud-seeding techniques?

LIZ in Hastings

BRUCE from Penistone
Bio-meteorologist

You can make it rain by spraying silver iodide into clouds, but it hasn't proven to be statistically effective on a grand scale. That said, there are over 2,000 weather manipulation stations in China alone.

Simon,

I have a large magnet and a small magnet in my toolbox at work, which I use for various tasks. The smaller of the magnets is the more powerful of the two.

Why are my magnets of different strengths? What determines the strength of a magnet?

WAYNE in Prospect

PETE from Sheffield
Works at a magnet company

The small magnet will be a rare-earth magnet with high 'energy product', whereas the weaker, larger one will be ferrite. Permanent magnets are just that and won't become unmagnetized unless they are purposely de-magged. Many properties affect magnetic strength.

> Simon,
>
> *How far away from the earth's surface does gravity stop, and why does it stop?*
>
> **SOPHIE,** *aged 7, in Irvine*

STEVE from Hayes
Physicist

Gravity is infinite – it just diminishes to almost nothing the further away from earth you get.

> Dear Simon,
>
> I have to build a pressure rocket using a bottle, which I will then demonstrate in science class.
> I have tried many methods proposed on the internet, but none seems to work brilliantly.
> Can you help me find the best design?
>
> **CHARLIE** in **Marlborough**

JAMES from Llanishen School in Cardiff
Science teacher

 Drill a hole in a cork and insert it in a pop bottle that's half full of water. Put a bike valve through the hole and pump it with the bike pump. After a while, the pressure will send it sky high.

Simon,

Is the volume of water on the planet the same today as it's ever been? Do we keep reusing the same water?

Thank you!

LESLIE

PETER from Marlborough
CEO of a sustainable company

The amount of water on the earth is the same as when life began. It simply re-disperses itself. Seventy per cent of the earth's surface is water. Of that, 2.5 per cent is fresh water, and only 1 per cent of *that* is fit for human consumption.

Simon,

Quite simply – how many people are on the planet right now?

AMY

NICOLA from Bristol
Geography teacher

The current population stands at just over 7 billion and is increasing all the time, although growth is slowing. Organizations like the UN compile all the data they get from each country and make estimates of the overall population. But it is only approximate.

> Simon,
>
> The other day my 11-year-old daughter Daisy was engaging me in one of those ridiculous conversations where she just says 'Why?' to whatever I say.
>
> She ended up asking me why plants die, and I was completely stumped. Is there a reason for plants having a lifespan?
>
> **SARAH-JANE** in Penryn

BARBARA from Watford
Geneticist

As plants grow, cells divide and the DNA has to copy itself. But each time it reproduces, it doesn't copy quite as well, until eventually it doesn't work.

Simon,

We were in the car when my 7-year-old son Ben asked: 'What makes glass see-through?' I really have no idea.

ANNIE in Bradford

GORDON from Largs
BSc in chemistry, and former head of technical support at a glass company

Normal clear glass is transparent because none of the chemical elements present in it absorb significant amounts of visible radiation (i.e. light).

Hi Simon,

I'm on holiday in Wales and, after visiting many rural places, I was wondering why Wales has so much slate.

Thank you!

LIAM, aged 13, in North Wales

ROB from Bedfordshire
Secondary school head of geology

Half a billion years ago, Wales was covered by deep ocean, and this low-energy water allowed very fine mud to settle. Over time it was squashed into mudstone or shale. Plate tectonic activity resulted in the landmass of Scotland smashing into Wales and England and the pressure turned the shale into metamorphic rock, slate.

Simon,

I discovered today that J.K. Rowling has sold
400 million books. While I appreciate that this is a
fantastic achievement, I wondered how many trees
would be needed to make that many books.

BARRY in Henlow

KEVIN from Aberdeenshire
Group environmental adviser for a paper company

There's no way of telling *exactly* how many trees have
been cut down. Many books, including the Harry
Potter series, use Forest Stewardship Certified paper,
which is far more environmentally friendly and would
result in the loss of fewer trees.

> Simon,
>
> *I was doing a world jigsaw with my five-year-old daughter Martha, when she wondered how different the world would be if it spun in the other direction.*
>
> **DAVID** in Sidcup

MATT from Brattleby
Physics student

The sun would rise in the west, and set in the east. The stars would read differently – the sequence in which stars are currently mapped would be inverted. Moonrise would also be inverted. Additionally, clockwise would be anti-clockwise, and vice versa, such as on sundials.

Hi Simon,

We've just moved to a house with a large garden and a pond. I say pond, but I like to call it a lake, as it's 40 metres long by 20 metres wide, has a small jetty, and a floating duck house in the middle.

So am I justified in calling it a lake? When does a pond become a lake?

MARTIN in Cuckfield

BEV from Bognor Regis
Pond survey officer

The definition of a pond is a water body with a surface area between 1 square metre and 2 hectares, which holds water for 4 months of the year or more.

Hi Simon,

I'd like to know why an iron is the only appliance that doesn't have an on/off switch. Why can you only switch it off at the wall?

VANESSA in Northumberland

SIMON from Coleford
Electrician

The logic is not to have an on/off switch on the body of the iron as it's an electrical appliance that houses water, and any damage or wearing down of such a switch could lead to an ingress of water and possibly electrocution.

Simon,

Toby, my 7-year-old son, asked me, 'What is a flame made of?' I'm 43 and have no idea. Can you or your listeners help?

Thank you!

TOBY'S MUM in Kent

COLIN from Fleet
Works for the Defence Fire Service

 When you see flame spark, you are watching a process called pyrolization. Everything has a temperature at which it burns. When it starts to break down, it emits gases, and this in combination with oxygen and heat are what creates the flame. So, in short, it depends what you're burning as to what's in the flame.

Simon – please help!

If I were to go to the North Pole, and stand at the very top of the world, I imagine South would be a whole 360 degrees around me. But is it actually directly below me? And how would I be able to judge where East and West begin?

NICK in Weston-super-Mare

PHIL
Pilot

It's a nightmare, but you need a polar stereographic chart. This flattens out the landscape and enables you to take grid references. Everything is indeed south if you're on the pole.

Simon,

Can you help me with this question?
If you turn the volume up on your TV, or make it brighter, or access the Teletext, or use other features, does it use more electricity?

ALISON in Sudbury

MICHAEL from Ampthill
Power-tests televisions for a living

If you increase the brightness on television sets it does use up extra energy in *most* cases. If you increase the volume on a television set it uses up extra energy but only by a small amount. Using Teletext makes very little difference to the energy consumption at all.

> *Simon,*
>
> *This is a question that's puzzled me since a school trip to the Lake District when I was 11 – when it comes to maps, what are the boundary lines for the land, the beach and the sea? And does it matter if the tide is in or out?*
>
> *Thanks!*
>
> ### CHRISTINE in Cromford

ALAN from Bristol
Mountain Rescue incident controller

'Tide gauge zero' is where the land meets the sea, as defined by cartographers.

The UK fundamental tide gauge benchmark is 7.801 metres above this; this is used on marine charts.

Ordnance Survey maps are based on the datum at Newlyn in Cornwall, which is 3.05 metres above tide gauge zero.

Simon,

How long does grass live? Is it everlasting, and what's the oldest grass in the UK?

PAUL

GLEN from Gorefield
Ecologist

Depends on the species. Annual grasses only grow one year. Perennials tend to be 5–10 years. Bamboos, meanwhile, are grasses and live for hundreds of years.

Simon,

While looking at a rainbow, I started to wonder how big it was. What is the radius of the average rainbow? How do you measure it?

Thanks!

DALE in Guildford

HOLLY from London
BBC weather forecaster

A rainbow is a band of colours caused by light refracting off water droplets. The rainbow will appear larger and longer depending on the angle of view. However, as its size is always subjective, a rainbow is impossible to measure.

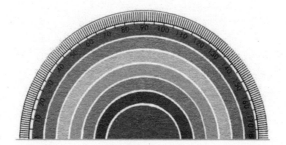

Dear Simon,

The clocks move back at the end of October, roughly eight weeks before the winter solstice. So, by rights, shouldn't they move forward again at the end of February, eight weeks after the solstice?

Thank you,

MATTHEW

DOC from Tunbridge

The clocks change around the equinox, and not the solstice, as this signifies the change when days become longer or shorter than the nights.

Hi Simon,

My 11-year-old daughter Leah has noticed that when you put the kettle on it gets quieter just before it comes to the boil. Why is that?

IAN in Leicester

BARRY in North Wales
Former nuclear reactor engineer

 The noise you can hear is the heat bubbles bursting. When the water around them becomes hot enough, as the kettle comes to the boil, they stop bursting – so the kettle becomes less noisy just before switching off.

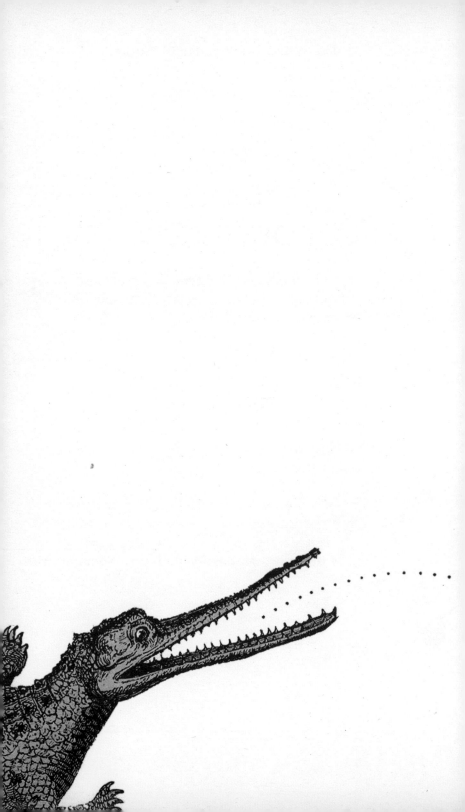

'CAN CROCODILES SPIT?'

Animal Antics

> *Dear Simon,*
>
> *When geese are flying south for the winter (or, indeed, on the way back) in that familiar V-formation – who decides who's at the front? Is it the same one each time, or do they take it in turns?*
>
> *Hope you can help!*
>
> **BRIAN** in Colchester

PETER from Slimbridge
Head of species recovery at a conservation organization

The goose at the front is the one doing most of the work. The others follow in a V-formation, riding on the slipstream of the bird in front, and therefore expending less energy. When the leader gets tired he'll slip back in the formation to take advantage of the slipstream himself.

If a youngster is ill and drops out of the formation, its family members tend to drop out also.

Simon,

I have a simple question which I'm hoping you can help me with.

Last week our two goldfish died, which got my sister and me thinking – do they have ears? And can they hear what we do?

LAURA in Mawsley

PAUL from Bridgend
Has kept tropical fish for 30 years

Fish don't have ears, but they can hear. They have a lateral line, from behind the gills to their tail, which allows them to feel the pressure waves in water – therefore giving them a sort of hearing.

Our eardrums work because air pressure waves move them. It's similar for fish, but their hearing comes more from movement in water.

Simon,

Every summer there is a particular spot in my back garden where midges gather. It happens to be at an area that we always have to walk through.

Why is this, and is there any way of getting rid of them?

KATH in Falmouth

ALAN
Chairman of Buglife, the Invertebrate Conservation Trust

Midges tend to swarm in sheltered areas, as they are weak flyers and keen to stay out of the wind. Hence, for example, they might gather under tree branches. Assembly areas could also be good markers, enabling them to get their bearings.

The midges that swarm are likely to be males waiting for females to come along.

Don't get rid of them – let them be!

Simon,

Why do owls hoot? Owls are designed to fly as silently as possible to surprise their prey, and they are solitary birds. Last night between about three and four o'clock I heard an owl hooting nearby. I'm sure if I was a mouse I would have hidden!

MAUREEN in Ruthin

EDDIE from Groombridge
Works at the Raptor Centre, the UK's oldest sanctuary for birds of prey

The only UK owls that hoot are tawny owls. They hoot in order to declare the ownership of their territory, and warn other owls away. They won't hoot when they are hunting! They hunt by stealth.

Simon,

For many years I've been greatly puzzled by this question – how does a chameleon know it's blending in with its surroundings? Is the colour change a natural process or a conscious decision by the chameleon?

Thank you!

LINDSAY *near Milton Keynes*

DAVE from Gwenddwr
Works with the 'Rainforest Roadshow'; he's also just returned from Madagascar

It's a myth that chameleons change colour to suit their surroundings. They actually alter their skin tone according to their mood. There are different species of chameleon whose natural colour usually matches their habitat.

Simon,

This morning at about 6.30 a.m. a flock of birds – Canada geese possibly – flew past my house in a southerly direction, presumably flying south for the winter.

I wonder, do they always fly on a particular day/weekend? The weather has been summery, so surely it can't be that they sense it is getting colder.

SALLY in Marden

MICHAEL from Adlington
Amateur birdwatcher

Birds do have internal clocks that tell them when to start their migration, regardless of the weather day-to-day. The clocks vary for different birds, so some may leave earlier than others.

However, if the birds you saw flying past your house were Canada geese, they weren't migrating – they are feral birds, which means they don't migrate – they'd just be moving locally.

Simon,

My 2¹/₂-year-old is at the stage where he finds his tummy button intriguing. He recently asked me where our cat's tummy button is. Do other animals have tummy buttons, or is it just us humans?

ANTHONY in Belgium

SHARON from Taunton
Vet

All living beings are born with an umbilical cord. Most animal mothers bite it off at birth, allowing the wound to heal over. But humans tie them and clip them to avoid infection, meaning it heals as a lump of tissue – which is why the tummy button's visible for us and not other animals.

Simon,

On holiday in Australia recently I was the preferred meal for what felt like every mosquito in the entire state. But I know people who never get bitten, and most get just one or two bites. Why are some people targeted more than others? And can anything be done to avoid this?

LORNA in Glasgow

DR BROMLEY from Colchester
Lecturer in clinical physiology and expert in travel medicine

There's no official proof that they bite some people more than others, but we do know mosquitoes are attracted to heat, carbon dioxide and body odours. These can all be imperceptible to us, but some people emit more than others.

Simon,

Moths only come out at night, and then they head straight for the nearest source of light – usually my house, if the window is open. Why don't they come out during the day? Then we'd all be happy.

TONY in Harpenden

DAVID from Weston-super-Mare
Lepidopterist

Moths mainly fly at night so they don't get eaten by birds. They use the moon as a navigational aid, and they're attracted to light because it has some of the qualities of the moon.

> *Simple question, Simon: how and why do cats purr?*
>
> *Thank you!*
>
> **EMMA** *in St Austell*

PHILIP from Brighton
Veterinary surgeon

 They have folds of skin in their larynx which vibrate when they breathe both in and out. When they experience a heightened emotion, such as happiness, fear, anger or arousal, the vibrations increase massively, creating the purring sound.

Simon,

We keep six ex-battery chickens: Babs, Bruce, Gnasher, Scrawny, Ducky and Hattie. Babs, Gnasher and Bruce lay beautiful eggs regularly, while Ducky lays eggs daily but forgets to add the shell, so the egg is enclosed only in the membrane.

My wife Angie has to hang around the coop very early every morning to catch Ducky's egg as soon as she lays it, to stop the others eating it. They are fed on meal, some corn, and plenty of greenery. We also add calcium supplement to their feed to help with eggshell production.

How can we persuade Ducky to add the shell to her eggs?

TONY in New Zealand, Wiltshire

ALISON from Addlethorpe
Has a breeding flock of 70 and has also had rescue chickens

You need to feed them poultry grit, which is basically crushed-up seashell. It helps replace the calcium, which they draw from their own body.

Simon,

How high can a fly fly?

TIM

ANDY from Birmingham
Skydiver

 I've hit one at about 6,000 feet, but they struggle beyond 8,000 feet if they get stuck in your helmet.

Hi Simon,

The other day, my 6-year-old son Thomas asked me, 'When it's night-time, do fish go to sleep?'

I paused for a moment, before answering, 'I don't know. But I know a man who can find out. We should ask Simon Mayo.'

'Why should we ask Simon Mayo?' was his reply.

'Because he can find out the answer to all sorts of things, including your fish question,' I said.

'Oh, OK then,' came his satisfied response.

So, over to you, Simon!

LINDA in Gravesend

PETER from Manchester
Diver for 30 years

Yes, they do, but in different ways, and not in the same way as we humans. Some will rest on the tides, others lie on the bottom, while still others conceal themselves in the rocks.

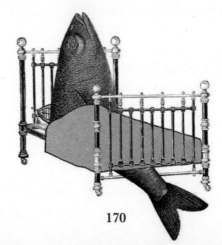

Hi Simon,

My border terrier, Ivy, loves to sniff out rabbits. In the process of doing this, she occasionally sticks her head in stinging nettles. However, she shows no sign of being stung.

So to my question: is it possible for dogs to be stung on the nose? Or does she just have a high pain threshold, as dogs are supposed to have?

CAROLINE in Somerset

HEDLEY from Penrith
Working with gundogs for 40 years

It is possible for dogs to be stung, the key areas being the inside of the ear, the nose and the pads of the feet. They are clearly irritated by this, too.

SIMON from Bristol
Dog-owner with nettle patch at end of garden

My dog is very much affected by stings, and reacts and scratches whenever up against the nettles in the patch.

Hello Simon,

After inadvertently trapping a honey bee in the cab of my delivery van, I began to wonder how far from its hive it could travel before no longer being able to find its way home. And what does it do with its collected pollen? Can it be dropped off at any other hive?

ADRIAN in Leeds

BRYAN from Aylesbury
Bee-whisperer and fourth-generation beekeeper

The longest recorded flight of a bee from its hive is 15 miles. A female bee will travel as far as it needs to in order to gather pollen, and will only travel far if the rewards are bountiful.

If a female bee returns to a foreign hive, she will normally get turned away by the residents, depending on whether she is carrying pollen. Male bees, on the other hand, can enter any hive they wish.

Simon,

I was walking along a beach in Cornwall, and I was amazed at the number of starfish that had been washed up. They appeared to be dead, and I picked them up and put them in my bucket with some seawater. A while later, most of them were showing signs of life.

My question is, how long can a starfish survive out of water?

SIAN in Portland

DR HOBSON from Swansea University
Marine biologist

We make the assumption that if a starfish is stranded on the high spring tide, it will be dead by the time the tide comes back in. So, in other words, less than 12 hours.

> Simon,
>
> The other day during dinner my 4-year-old asked me, 'Mummy, do ants sneeze?' She went on to specify that her question was regarding red ants.
> I am stumped. Can you help?
>
> **VICTORIA** in South Wales

ROB from Alsager
Studied horticulture, which included invertebrate zoology

Ants (and insects generally) don't sneeze. They don't have lungs, and therefore don't take in oxygen in the same way as mammals. They take in oxygen through spiracles, small holes in their abdomen.

Simon,

Our chicken coop has been richly rewarded for the last few months with up to five eggs a day from our six chickens. The past two days, though, one of the girls has been laying eggs with a strange green tint to them.

Can anyone explain what this means, and whether the eggs are edible?

Many thanks!

KIM in Stoke Climsland

ROGER from Upottery
Chicken breeder

The chicken must have been interbred at some stage with an Arucana, a South American chicken. The Arucana lays eggs that have a green-blue tint.

Simon,

I've been stewing over a puzzle that neither my dad, my physics teacher nor my geography teacher can answer – when lightning strikes the sea, why don't all the fish die?

Thanks!

HANNIE in the New Forest

DAVID
Masters in fish biology

Some fish could very well be affected, though they would need to have been immediately under the lightning strike! As seawater is highly conductive, the electricity will dissipate rapidly after impact.

Hello Simon,

I take my dog to training classes – she's a springer/lab cross. However, despite doing all our homework, I have problems keeping her attention for any length of time, even with treats. How can I solve this, and how can I stop her wanting to chase sheep, squirrels, and so on?

Thanks!

GILLIAN in Hathern

EMMA from Barns Green
Dog behaviourist

Dogs don't understand treats. You have to be more alpha with her. Discipline her with stern tones and a gentle tap on the side, as dogs do when they discipline each other. It's all about creating hierarchy, with you at the top.

Simon,

When my grandson and I take the dog for a walk, we often walk through spiders' threads stretched across the path. Sometimes the distance between the anchor points of these threads is 15 to 20 feet, so my question is: how do they spin the first thread over such long distances? And what are they hoping to catch?

Thanks!

BOB in Gateshead

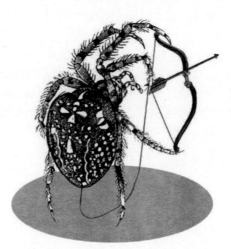

RAY

Member of the British Tarantula Society

 There are two possible scenarios:

1) Young spiders do something called ballooning – once hatched, they climb to the highest point, and allow a little trail of silk. The wind catches the silk, and takes the spider with it, which is what you may be walking through.

2) Spiders can spin webs of incredible size – they tie a piece of silk to a point on one tree, and then climb down the tree trailing silk as they go, walk on to the next tree, climb up, and then have a length of web that bridges the gap.

Simon,

I drive home from work in Swindon, in the dark, in the middle of January, along Wiltshire's leafy lanes to my home in the hamlet of New Zealand, which nestles cosily against the perimeter fence of RAF Lyneham.

I prefer to use the lanes, rather than the main road, because I arrive home more relaxed and ready to withstand the onslaught of school homework, and personal problems faced by my 17-year-old daughter.

The question is, why, as I drive home in the middle of January, am I bombarded with moths? Surely moths should be hibernating, or dead, or waiting for last year's eggs to hatch into this year's adults? Can anybody explain why the lanes I drive along are filled with moths?

TONY in New Zealand, Wiltshire

MATTHEW
Lepidopterist and entomologist

They are most likely winter moths, although there are several other species that survive the winter months. Only male winter moths fly – females are wingless. They're everywhere, and they come out to fill an ecological niche.

> Simon,
>
> *I can understand why cats would chase mice, as they will catch them, play with them and possibly eat them. But I can't see a dog catching a cat and eating it. So, where does this 'dog chases cat, cat runs away from dog' instinct come from?*
>
> *Why do dogs chase cats?*
>
> **GRAHAM** in Fakenham

JULIE from Lakenheath
Greyhound trainer

Dogs are basically domesticated wolves and have a very strong hunting instinct. If they see something running away, cat or otherwise, they'll chase after it. We harness this instinct when we train them to race.

Simon,

Can a bird of one species understand the birdsong or calls of a bird from a different species? For example, can a blackbird understand the song of a robin or a thrush?

If any of your very intelligent listeners know the answer, I would love to find out.

CHARLIE

SEAN from Burton-on-Trent
Been birdwatching since 1979

The question should rather be what calls do different birds respond to. Virtually all birds will respond to alarm calls, but they will not respond to song calls, as these are designed to attract a mate.

Simon,

Why don't pet food manufacturers make mouse- or bird-flavoured cat food?

Thanks!

DIANNE in Carnforth

ABIGAIL from Waltham on the Wolds
Works at a centre for pet nutrition

 Flavour is accompanied by nutritional value – so we use real chicken, and that's healthy for the cat. But it's also about sustainability – we're not in the business of farming mice and sparrows.

> Simon,
>
> My five-year-old came home from school yesterday, horrified at some of her classmates' spitting habits. This prompted the question, 'Can crocodiles spit?'
>
> Thanks!
>
> **POLLY** in Kent

TONY from Burgess Hill
RSPCA inspector and former zookeeper

Crocodiles can't spit, but there are plenty of animals that can, including archer fish and llamas.

To Simon and the team,

My dog rolled in a dead rat recently, and really enjoyed it. Why did he do this, and why do dogs want to smell so bad? What does this smell like to them?

GAVIN

ROSIE in Jersey
Clinical companion animal behaviourist

There are several theories. One is that they are camouflaging themselves – to cover their own scent. Another is that they are self-medicating, to get rid of parasites from their fur. A more recent theory is that they do it to carry the scent back to other dogs, to show off to them.

> Hi Simon,
>
> We've just got two new kittens – Ron, a male tabby, and Pam, a female tortoiseshell.
>
> Apparently more tortoiseshell cats are girls and more ginger cats are boys. My kids Alice, eight, and George, five, want to know why. Can you or one of your insightful listeners help?
>
> **JESSICA** in Toddington

LIZ in Kendal
Vet

Just like in humans, female cats have XX chromosomes, and males have XY chromosomes. As well as determining the sex of the cat, these also determine its colour. Only the X chromosome can carry colour genes. Since a male cat only has one X chromosome, he's either got the ginger gene or he hasn't. The colour of the fur of the female cat is more complicated. She can have colour information on both Xs, and one might override the other, but not always consistently. So if she has ginger on one X and brown on the other X, she will have patches of ginger and brown in her fur – a tortoiseshell. A male tortoiseshell is very, very rare (but never say never in Nature). A female ginger is not so rare, however. If she carries ginger genes on both Xs, she will be ginger, just like the ginger tom. She is, however, outnumbered by the ginger tom by about three or four to one. This is why female cats can have more than one colour and males can't. And that's why female cats of only one colour are outnumbered.

Simon,

It's a playground question, but after we'd discussed it in the office we decided to throw this open to the experts: hippo versus rhino – who wins?

Thanks!

SIMON in Southampton

CHRIS from Chelmsford
Witnessed the aftermath of a hippo–rhino face-off!

I was on a game reserve in Zambia. The ranger recounted the story, saying that the rhino had found itself between the mother hippo and her baby. A fight broke out and the hippo won. Bear in mind, rhinos are very short-sighted, and hippos have 3-foot-long teeth.

Hippos have a reputation for being particularly fierce when confronted – even lions and crocodiles steer clear!

'HOW CAN
I MAKE A CHAMPION
CONKER?'

Random Ruminations

> *Simon,*
>
> *Who decided that emergency cars (police, ambulance, etc.) should have blue flashing lights, and not any other colour?*
>
> **VINCE** in Bracknell

ELLIS from Seaton
A-level science student

Blue light enters the retina quicker than any other colour of the spectrum, meaning the brain recognizes it before any other colour. That's why it is used by the emergency services – to get your attention!

> *Simon,*
>
> *I came away from a recent visit to Winchester Cathedral with a burning question. How much would it cost to build said or similar cathedral in all its glory today, and how long would it take?*
>
> **CHRIS** in Yateley

MAXWELL
Architect

It would cost huge amounts of money, bearing in mind that a school costs £20–25 million. It's really impossible to put a figure on it. I've just come back from Rome, where reconstruction of the burned-down basilica in the Vatican took forty years, although that was at the turn of the last century and using old techniques. Guildford Cathedral took about seven years to reconstruct in the 1920s, but that was with more modern equipment and materials. Sagrada Familia in Barcelona hasn't even been finished yet – they've been building that for 130 years.

Simon,

I have a PE project to design a sports stadium. It can be made of anything, but needs to be eco-friendly. Please help!

STAN

MARK from Plymouth
Sustainable construction manager

Refurbish an existing stadium, don't build a new one. Use recycled products such as crushed tyres for the running track. Think of cool gizmos, like chairs that create energy when they're raised and lowered.

> Simon,
>
> When people fire guns into the air in celebration, what happens to the bullets? How far into the air do they go, and do they hurt anybody when they come back down to earth?
>
> **CHRIS** in Penzance

PETER from Scarborough
Ex-army officer and armaments expert

When you fire a gun in the air, the bullets come down pretty much as hard as they go up. It is really, really dangerous – if one hits you it will kill you.

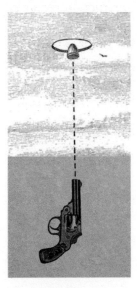

Simon,

My car stereo volume goes up to 64. My last car went to 63. How are volume numbers decided? And why don't they round them up or down?

TONY in Belper

PHIL from Lindford
Sound engineer

The numbers represent nothing – they're completely arbitrary!

Simon, can you help with my homework?
I need to create a music composition in G Major for my music GCSE, which starts next week. I've left it to the last minute, as usual, and don't have a clue where to start!

ELLEN, aged 14,
  in Weston-super-Mare

BOB from Hythe
Musician and music teacher, with an MA in Music Performance

Create a little chord sequence in G, C and D. Throw in an E minor if you want to get a little complicated. Record it on to something then play it back, and experiment with the notes from the G major scale – any of those notes should create a melody over the sequence.

Simon,

Where do postcodes come from? Who decides the postcode for a particular area in the first place, particularly the second part of the code? Are they just random numbers and letters chosen by a computer, or is there a system?

PHIL in Tunbridge Wells

ANDREW from Chorley
Used to work for Royal Mail

There is a system. The first letters represent the town, the next two numbers the postal sorting office (say, Bude 23). The start of the second part is the rural/town area. The last two letters are the walk/house/street. Royal Mail did all this manually.

Simon, please help!!

I'm doing a history assignment, and all I need is a figure for how many witch trials there were in England, Germany and Spain between 1560 and 1660. I've been searching for two days, and am slowly losing the will to live . . .

LAUREN in Bridport

ROBERT from Ohio
Professor of history

Far and away the most were in Germany. During that period, I estimate there were 75,000 trials and 35,000 executions altogether. Only 500 or so were in England and 1,000 or so in Spain, and the rest were in Germany.

Dear Simon and team,

I was having a clear-out the other day, and in the back of a cupboard I found a few bottles of unopened aftershave that must be at least ten years old.

They still smell OK to me, but it got me wondering how long fragrance keeps if unopened. Shall I use them, or would it be better to throw them out?

Thanks!

DANNY

STEVIE from Oxford
Chemist

Fragrances are a mix of chemicals. Some are designed to smell nice, others are designed to hide unpleasant odours in the compound. Both of these will degrade with time. So either the scent will cease to smell as pungent, or it will start to smell unpleasant. Most companies expect the shelf life to be around two years. But if you still like the smell, keep wearing it!

Simon,

Some say freeze them, some say varnish them, some say bake them, some say soak them in vinegar . . . but what really is the best way to get that champion conker to crush all the opposition?

ROB *in* Colchester

JOHN
Secretary of the World Conker Championships

Competitors at our event can't bring their own, but have them chosen at random. However, I have heard contestants talk about vinegar, baking, keeping from year to year, and *even passing them through a pig!*

Hi Simon,

When I was a boy, watching Westerns at the cinema, I was always puzzled by why a moving stagecoach wheels went round the correct way, then sometimes appeared to go in reverse, and then, often in the same scene, appear not to rotate at all! I'm still baffled, several decades later. Do you know an expert who can explain this, please?

MIKE in West Riding

DON from Torquay
Videographer and photographer

It's all to do with the speed of the wheels compared to the speed of the frames. The typical speed of the frames is 25 per second. If the wheels are rotating faster or slower, they'll appear to be going backwards or forwards. If they are exactly aligned, they will appear stationary.

Dear Simon,

How do I learn my ballroom dance steps as a beginner, when between lessons my house really isn't big enough to practise in – I can't take more than four steps in any direction before bumping into the furniture!

Many thanks!

CLIVE in Brighton

REBECCA from Hereford
Dance teacher

As a beginner, you shouldn't need to take more than four steps. Get yourself a rug and master the basics on that rug. In the case of salsa, for instance, forward on right, back on left. I practise in my dining room, which is tiny, all the time.

To Simon,

We've recently moved to Scotland, and the twisty-turny roads have exposed the effect that my husband's and my driving styles have on our children – they plead with me to drive, as they don't feel sick when I do, but their dad gives them car sickness.

We drive at a similar speed, but I tend to use the gears more than my husband, going down to third on a bend that he'd happily take in fifth.

Can you explain the differing effects our driving styles have on our children?

VALERIE in Helensburgh

DR RUTLAND from Wokingham
Ex-anatomy lecturer and member of the Institute of Advanced Motorists

You're basically the better driver – slowing into the bends and accelerating smoothly out of them. The emetic centre in the brain controls the feelings of sickness. Poor drivers are more likely to affect the emetic centre, and thus make their passengers feel sick because their driving style is more jerky.

Simon,

When is an island not an island? The British Isles are islands, Cyprus is an island, but is Australia an island?

When does land surrounded by water become too big to be an island?

BENJAMIN, aged 9, in Aberdeen

NICOLA from Bristol
Geography teacher

The term island is generally considered to refer to a land mass entirely surrounded by water, but smaller than a continent. As Australia is a continent, it is often not considered to be an island – though it is sometimes dubbed 'the world's largest island'. It's not an exact science, though. It's also to do with size, tectonic plates and indigenous flora and fauna.

Simon,

Why are traffic lights the colours they are? What makes green safe and red dangerous?

NICK in Belfast

ADAM
Motoring journalist

 It appears we're taking our cue from nature, where red generally signifies danger, and green is the healthier option! They are found on ships, railways and roads.

SIMON
Life-long sailor

 Traffic lights are red and green because of the collision regulations at sea. If a ship sees a red (port navigation) light, it does not have the right of way; if it sees a green (starboard navigation) light, then it may proceed, as it does have the right of way.

> Simon,
>
> I've sat in motorway roadworks for hours looking at the 'average speed cameras', and I have frequently wondered how they work. Thousands of cars must pass them hourly – but how do the cameras actually monitor the speeds? And do they reset when the speed limit is lowered?
>
> **PAUL** in Bradford

LEE from Manchester
From Drivesafe (Greater Manchester Casualty Reduction Partnership)

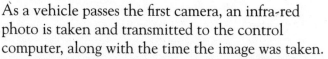

As a vehicle passes the first camera, an infra-red photo is taken and transmitted to the control computer, along with the time the image was taken.

As the vehicle passes the second camera, two pictures are taken – an infra-red photo and a colour photo. These are also transmitted to the control computer with the time they were taken.

The computer analyses the photos to retrieve the registration number of the vehicle.

The computer then compares the time of the two infra-red photos. These are used to calculate the speed of the vehicle between each camera.

If the speed is above the threshold, the information (speeds, date and time, vehicle registration, etc.) is written to disc, which is then checked by enforcement officers.

Dear Simon,

On the flight home from a recent holiday, when we were approaching to land, the cabin crew announced that they were going to dim the lights for safety reasons. I have also experienced this before take-off, when it's dark.

My question is: why? Surely the plane has enough power to take off or land without needing the lights off? Maybe a pilot or cabin crew member could help me out . . .

MATTHEW in Droitwich

MO

British Airways cabin crew for nearly 30 years

The reason cabin lights are dimmed for take-off and landing at night is because if – heaven forbid – there was to be an incident leading to an emergency evacuation, passengers' eyes would easily adjust to the lack of light outside the aircraft. If they went from a bright cabin to the dark sky, they wouldn't immediately be able to see any obstacles.

Hi Simon,

Where in the British Isles should I throw a 'message in a bottle' into the sea to have the best chance of the currents taking it the furthest, for discovery on a far-off foreign beach?

PAUL in Stroud

JOANNA in Bedford
Sailor who has just completed an 18,000-mile round-the-world race

The best place to drop the bottle would be Alderney in the Channel Islands. If you caught the 'Alderney Race' current between Alderney and Jersey, it could end up in the Bay of Biscay and eventually the West Indies.

Dear Simon,

This is a question from me and my kids.
  Where is the internet?
  It seems almost impossible to explain, but perhaps someone out there has a simple answer for us.

PAUL in Southampton

STUART in Thetford
Business systems analyst, working with computers for 15 years

The internet is everywhere! It's a network that connects millions of computers around the world. Each computer stores lots of information which the internet enables people, companies and organizations to share.

> Dear Simon,
>
> A simple question – I hope!
>   I would like to know if there is a bit of piano music that uses every single key (black and white) within the same piece.
>   Perhaps one of your musical listeners could help me out.
>
> ## CLARE in East Sussex

JAMES
Jazz club artistic director and a pianist

There is a piece of music that uses all the notes – it's called 'The Devil's Circus', and it's pretty horrible. It's a hard-driving piece that moves up and down the keys.

There's also another piece of music that has been performed, where a pianist played one single note (and held their finger on it) for a whole hour, before another came along and played the next (for another hour). It sounds a bit ridiculous, though . . .

> Simon,
>
> With the current economic climate, is there a country in the world that's totally debt-free?
>
> **JOHN** in London

BRIAN
Financial analyst

 There's more debt in the developed world than in the undeveloped. The latest reports suggest Liechtenstein and Brunei are among the very few countries without external debt, although they may have some debts of a slightly different kind.

'CAN A JELLYFISH STING ANOTHER JELLYFISH?'

Extra Homework

Simon,

Why are we encouraged to keep eggs in the fridge at home when supermarkets happily store them in normal shelves at room temperature? My fridge even has a special egg compartment that won't hold anything else . . .

Thank you!

SHARRON in Warrington

Hi Simon,

Why does my stainless steel cutlery sometimes come out with spots of rust on it from the dishwasher?

JAN in Welwyn

Dear Simon,

Every time I eat carrots I get the hiccups, particularly when they're raw. I have Googled this and found that many people also suffer from the same problem, but nobody can tell me why.

Please help!!

VICKY

Dear Simon,

Please could you help with my daughter Alice's dilemma, set by her Maths teacher? She has to find out how many chickens there are in the world and on average how many eggs they lay each day. Then she has to work out how many egg boxes they would fill (6 eggs in each box), and how many vans with a capacity of 3.4 cubic metres would be required to transport them. We have a week to work it out – help!

RAMMIE in Staffordshire

During a drive back from purchasing new shoes for the return to school the next day, my children were being exceptionally quiet in the back of the car.

My youngest, Zak, broke the silence. 'Mum?' he piped up. 'You know piranhas? Can they bite through crocodiles' teeth?'

To which I replied, 'I don't know. We'll ask Simon and the team.'

PAULA in the Cotswolds

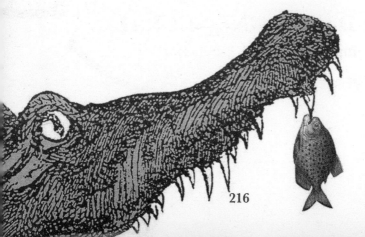

Dear Simon,

We are a group of archaeologists currently working in Lancaster. Our job is to analyze small pieces of flint and chert and classify them . . . it's very interesting if you're into that sort of thing, although anyone else might think we're completely insane!

However, we have uncovered a dilemma! There is a particular material called Tuffaceous Chert and none of us know what it is, nor does anyone else we've asked. Could anyone out there please help us? We know what Tuff is (material formed by being thrown out of a volcano) and we know what Chert is (silica-based stone formed by the silica leaching through limestone and into bedding layers) – but what is Tuffaceous Chert, how is it formed and why is called Tuffaceous Chert?!

Please help!

Yours,

DAVE, ANNE, MICHAL and *ANNE* in Lancaster

Hi Simon,

I can understand when listening to music that different notes are produced by different wavelengths, but what is the property of sound that enables us to distinguish different instruments (or voices) playing the same note?

Great show!

PETER

Dear Simon,

How does one stop deer eating one's garden plants? We've hung a large number of 'packets' of human hair in tights all along the hedge between our back garden and the horse paddock adjoining it, but we came home only today to find a deer happily sitting on our lawn and munching away.

Are there any deer experts out there who could help?

RIETTE in Poole

Simon,

I have to learn the Periodic Table off by heart in a week. Any tips?

Thanks,

JOSH in Somerset

Hi Simon,

Here's something that has puzzled me for a long time - is the Earth ever going to get too heavy? An acorn only weighs a couple of grams but it grows into a massive, heavy oak tree. Is it the case that when one tree grows another dies, balancing it out, or is there going to come a time when the Earth gets too heavy to support everything on it?

Thanks,

FIONA from Chichester

Hi Simon,

I was looking at a twenty-pound note recently and it made me wonder just how much money there is in the world altogether. Mum says not too much as everybody owes everybody else so much money. Please could you help?

Thanks very much,

AMY, aged 10, in Devon

Hi Simon,

While on holiday with my son Thomas, my wife Lisa and other friends, my son asked how much cloud there is in the sky. So that got me wondering what percentage of the earth is covered in cloud and what's the least amount of cloud there has ever been on earth?

ANDY in Champniers-et-Reilhac, France

Simon,

My youngest daughter, Charlotte, aged 7, asked a totally random question yesterday while in the car on the way back from the park.
'Can a jellyfish sting another jellyfish?'

Does anyone know?

RICHARD in Bangor

Simon,

My son, inspired by Brian Cox and Kate Humble's recent Orbit programme, asked me when was the last time all the planets were in line. Does anybody know? Also, when will they all be in line again?

Thanks,

MICHELLE in Kent

Hi Simon,

If everybody in Britain removed their money from the banks on the same day, would there be enough hard cold cash to give people? This question has been bugging me since I opened my first bank account and was surprised to find out my money wasn't actually in the downstairs vault!

CHRIS in Barnoldswick

Hi Simon,

Why can't we hear the earth rotating? Billions of tonnes of rock sloshing around under us seem to make no noise. Why not?

JOE from Norwich

Hi Simon,

I work for a Scottish Bank and the popular opinion amongst Scots is that their currency notes are 'legal tender' south of the border. Is this actually true? Is anyone in England obliged to accept Scottish notes, and for that matter, Irish bank notes? If not, why not? I've been asked this so many times, and I can't seem to find a definitive answer. Please help!

JEG in Oban

Hi Simon,

Whilst looking out of my kitchen window at the rain, I found myself wondering – if rain is clear, why are rainclouds black?

Thanks,

RACHEL in Coventry

Simon Mayo broadcasted on BBC Radio 1 for fifteen years, including presenting the breakfast show from 1988 to 1993. He followed this up by fronting the Radio Five Live afternoon show between 2001 and 2009. He also appeared on TV, with a presenting role on *Top of the Pops*, and was anointed as Bob Holness's heir apparent for the return of the phenomenally popular quiz show *Blockbusters* earlier this year. During his career Simon has won a string of awards, the latest being a Sony Award for his current *Drivetime* show on BBC Radio 2.